All Systems Go

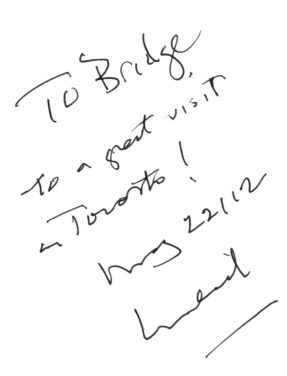

To Bridge,

To a great visit
in Toronto!

22/12

All Systems Go

The Change Imperative for Whole System Reform

Michael Fullan

Foreword by Peter Senge

A JOINT PUBLICATION

For information:

Corwin
A SAGE Company
2455 Teller Road
Thousand Oaks, California 91320
(800) 233-9936
Fax: (800) 417-2466
www.corwin.com

SAGE Ltd.
1 Oliver's Yard
55 City Road
London EC1Y 1SP
United Kingdom

SAGE India Pvt. Ltd.
B 1/I 1 Mohan Cooperative
    Industrial Area
Mathura Road,
    New Delhi 110 044
India

SAGE Asia-Pacific Pte. Ltd.
33 Pekin Street #02-01
Far East Square
Singapore 048763

Printed in the United States of America.

Library of Congress Cataloging-in-Publication Data

Fullan, Michael.
All systems go : the change imperative for whole system reform/Michael Fullan ; foreword by Peter Senge; A Joint publication with the Ontario Principals' Council.
      p. cm.
Includes bibliographical references and index.
ISBN 978-1-4129-7873-6 (pbk.)
    1. Educational change. 2. Educational planning. 3. School improvement programs. I. Title.

LB2806.F788 2010
371.2'07—dc22   2009051373

This book is printed on acid-free paper.

        11   12   13   14   10   9   8   7   6   5   4   3

Acquisitions Editor:	Arnis Burvikovs
Editorial Assistant:	Joanna Coelho
Production Editor:	Cassandra Margaret Seibel
Copy Editor:	Adam Dunham
Typesetter:	C&M Digitals (P) Ltd.
Proofreader:	Susan Schon
Indexer:	Jean Casalegno
Cover Designer:	Michael Dubowe

Contents

Foreword   vii
Peter Senge

Preface   xiii

Acknowledgments   xvii

About the Author   xxi

PART I. The System   1

1. **The Idea and Importance of Whole-System Reform**   3

2. **Deceptive Inadequacies**   19

PART II. Getting There   33

3. **Collective Capacity at the School and District Level**   35

4. **The State We Are In**   61

5. **Individual Capacity Building**   81

PART III. A New Era   93

6. **Politicians and Professionals Unite**   95

References   103

Index   107

Foreword

Are We Ready to Get Serious?

Peter Senge

A merica has been trying to turn around its schools for a quarter century, with tragic results. One simplistic quick-fix nostrum after another has seized the political limelight and been "driven" through the system as if it was all that was needed: decentralized site accountability, small high schools, high-stakes testing. While all these efforts embodied ideas with merit, the belief in one-size-fits-all fixes might itself be the real problem.

Michael Fullan has built an international reputation over the past decade for his work in England, Canada, and many other countries for helping educators, communities, and business and political leaders cooperate for systemic change in education. He has shown that unless you align school, district, state, and national agendas, innovation within schools cannot be sustained. He has shown that teachers and principals are more than ready to lead the innovation, but they must be part of larger learning communities aimed at building collective capacity across schools and school systems, rather than heroes and heroines fighting a dysfunctional system. He has shown that a few well thought out strategic priorities that encapsulate what we believe collectively about the fundamental aims for education are vital to establish a direction toward which everyone can work together. He has shown that accountability matters but only in the context of nurturing the overall esprit de corps within a school and community and tapping the huge reservoir of latent responsibility that exists with a nation's educators, parents, and community leaders. Put in the negative, beating educators with the you-need-to-be-more-accountable stick accomplishes little and may actually lead to less real accountability rather than more.

In short, Fullan has shown that real change is possible but only by taking a truly systemic approach. No single quick fixes. No good guy–bad guy politicizing to mobilize public anger. No fear mongering about America's declining competitiveness in the world. Just clear strategy, broad engagement (especially including educators themselves), and a consistent message that this can only be done by all of us working together across all levels of the educational system.

Where a whole-system approach has been taken seriously over the past decade, there have been significant improvements in student achievement. In the UK, with focused leadership starting with Tony Blair and Michael Barber, former director of the prime minister's educational reform effort, literacy and numeracy achievement rose from about 62% to 75% (as measured by proficiency of 11-year-olds) from 1997–2001, an improvement that Fullan himself was asked to evaluate.

Building on the experience in England, Fullan became special advisor to Premier Dalton McGuinty in Ontario and helped to design and guide a whole-system strategy for the Ontario school system. Focusing on a small set of core priorities and using capacity building and partnership as a core strategy (specifically avoiding punitive accountability), literacy and numeracy have increased 13% at the elementary level since 2003, students passing mandated secondary literacy has risen from 65% to 81%, and high school graduation rates in a diverse province have gone from 68% to 77%. Ontario has recently added early learning (full-day integrated schooling) for all four- and five-year-olds.

Results like these in England and Canada, and in other countries like Finland, Singapore, and Korea, have become recognized around the world, and today many other countries are following similar paths. Huge challenges remain in all these settings but for many the journey is well underway.

Can this be done in America? Fullan describes the current work in a few U.S. school districts, but the examples are isolated.

Indeed one of the primary features of the U.S. is wide disparities in educational attainment against a backdrop of steady decline overall. While we have many outstanding schools and districts, our overall performance as a nation in public education has fallen from the top in world rankings a half century ago (highest high school qualification in the world in 1960). Today, America consistently ranks in the bottom half of advanced (OECD) countries in educational achievement. The decline has continued unabated through the past decade: the U.S. was still number one in postsecondary graduation rates in 1995; it was number 14 by 2005. All of this has occurred despite a quadrupling of total funds spent on education since 1980 and spending more per pupil than any other school system.

In essence, we have thrown more money at more ineffective reform agendas than any nation. In so doing, we have shown a virtually inexhaustible penchant for using supposed educational reform to feather political nests and, as with other crucial national issues, a tragic inability to subordinate special interests to common good.

Beyond statistical comparisons to other countries, the consequences have been devastating at human and societal levels. For over a decade it has been more likely that a young African American boy growing up in an American city will go to prison than to any form of post-secondary education. A recent study found that only 35% of Boston's high school *graduates who had enrolled in college* in 2000 had actually completed either a two- or four-year college program seven years later. A recent McKinsey study estimates that the enormous educational disparities in America impose the "equivalent of a permanent national recession."

Thus, there is no shortage of evidence of the cost to America of how our present educational system operates. Yet, it was precisely evidence and statistics like these that motivated past quickfix reforms. So, they are not likely to suffice to mobilize the sort of cooperative whole-system effort Fullan proposes.

What could? I believe two things.

First, we must believe that real change is possible. My own experience is that public school educators in America are among the most beleaguered professionals. For years, I have asked diverse audiences whether or not they think a crisis is needed for systemic change. My point has been to get people thinking about their implicit models of change, and specifically whether they believe they can cultivate the aspiration and co-inspiration needed, in my opinion, to sustain change beyond simply reacting to a crisis. My experience in diverse audiences, however, is that the majority express the belief that, indeed, a crisis is needed, that no real change occurs without a crisis. I have always viewed this as an unfortunate commentary on our limited understanding of systemic change, of our reliance on desperation rather than aspiration. But the most unfortunate of all have been the groups of educators who often fail to raise their hands to either option. When I first encountered this, I asked the group in surprise, "Help me understand. I thought I asked an 'either-or' question: is a crisis needed for change, yes or no. How come most of you have not raised your hands for either option?" A quiet voice from the middle of the audience responded, "We don't believe that change is possible under any condition."

This is where work like Fullan's could be pivotal.

As you read the many examples here of engaging the variety of actors needed to truly rethink and recreate our schools, of fostering collaboration among teachers and students to build collective capacity, of people achieving significantly higher performance and real innovation, it is hard not to start to believe there are viable paths forward. Fullan's stories remind us that no one wants to be part of a low-performing system, including educators and students. Transforming the fatalism that currently afflicts far too many starts with a conviction that change is possible with a clear framework and practical tools for engagement and moving forward. It will then take politically savvy strategies to mobilize the diverse blocks of power that need to work better together, which is exactly what Fullan shows can be done.

But I believe there is a second factor that goes beyond change strategy. At no time in history has there been a more powerful need for a new vision of the purpose of education. Today's schools were born in the early stages of the industrial era. That is why they were organized like an assembly line (Grade 1, Grade 2, Grade 3, etc.). That is why they were based on standardized timetables governing each part of the day (complete with bells and whistles on the walls), and fixed, rigid curricula delivered by teachers whose job was first and foremost to maintain control, much like an assembly-line foreman. The Industrial Age school arose as part and parcel of an industrial-age economy based on exploiting natural (and many would argue social) capital to create productive and financial capital. The Industrial Age is ending. Despite the fact that we burn more coal and produce more steel than ever before in human history, we also use one and one-third Earths today to support the consumer-driven global industrial machine—and the side effects of industrial growth, like climate change and the destruction of the oceans, are getting harder to ignore. The challenge of our time is not economic competitiveness. The challenge is to build not only "sustainable" but *regenerative* societies—ones that enhance natural and social capital.

This is a challenge that young people everywhere increasingly recognize, as indicated by the global movement among the young to reverse climate change, stop the destruction of species and ecosystems, and face honestly the widening gaps between rich and poor. The wheels are coming off the train of the global economic growth machine and young people sense this. But they have real questions whether or not their adult "leaders" do, as reflected in large numbers of young people who are pessimistic about the ongoing and largely unmet challenges like climate change, water, and the destruction of ecosystems. And they have real questions regarding what they can do, if anything.

No institution has a more crucial role to play in the historic changes coming than school because no institution has greater potential to impact how a society changes over the long term. How we educate our children shapes the future, because they in turn will be the ones who create that future. The growing gap between what they need to be able to understand (such as alternative cultures and social-technological-ecological systems) and to do (such as work collaboratively to solve complex interdependent problems) and what we have traditionally taught is the primary reason so many young people find school less and less relevant for their lives. And they are right.

This past spring, in a gathering organized by the St. Louis Chamber of Commerce as part of their "Sustainable St. Louis" campaign, a series of presentations were made by middle school and high school students. Many of the adults were shocked. Expecting to hear stories about what they were studying in their environment or civics classes, instead they heard stories of how the young people were busy transforming their communities. One 12-year-old girl told the story of how she and four classmates decided that their school needed to stop using fossil fuels and how they got a wind turbine installed. As she retold their saga of working with their science teacher to develop the initial analysis, with parents developing the engineering and financial details, and of then presenting their plan to their principal and eventually the mayor (twice!), the room of several hundred adults fell silent. She then showed a photograph of the operating wind turbine outside her school. As she stood calmly in front of the audience she posed a question. "We kids always hear that, 'You are the future.' We don't agree. We don't have 20 or 30 years to make the changes needed. We are ready now. Are you?"

In short, we must imagine a vision for school that is far more compelling than fixing a broken system. As it has been for all of human history (not just in the Industrial Age), education is how a society shapes its future. It needs to be where we reflect on and develop the sorts of capabilities that the society, the young people, will need in the future. Only when we recognize this need for real innovation will we tap the aspiration needed to give life to the sorts of strategies that Michael Fullan so ably illustrates can succeed.

The real question is, Are we serious enough to work together in favor of the schools our future is asking for? I have no doubt that the young people are.

Preface

If there is one thing that you should remember from page one and all the way through this book it is the concept of *collective capacity*. It is the key to *All Systems Go* and the component most likely to be neglected by policymakers. Collective capacity is when groups get better—school cultures, district cultures, and government cultures. The big collective capacity and the one that ultimately counts is when they get better conjointly—collective, collaborative capacity, if you like. Collective capacity generates the emotional commitment and the technical expertise that no amount of individual capacity working alone can come close to matching.

Prior to the 1997 election in Britain, when Tony Blair asked Michael Barber to join him in crafting a comprehensive strategy for improving literacy and numeracy in all primary schools in the country, they started down the path of all systems go. For a while, upon being elected they had the knack of whole-system reform. From 1997 to 2001, literacy and numeracy achievement rose substantially from about 62% to 75% (as measured by proficiency of 11-year-olds). Quite an accomplishment, as we are talking about over 20,000 primary schools. In his second term, 2001 to 2005, with a large majority, Blair got distracted with other matters and lost the plot in educational reform, although his government did go on to do interesting things in public sector reform as described in Sir Michael's fascinating account, *Instruction to Deliver* (2008).

Along came Dalton McGuinty in 2002 as if on cue. Leader of the opposition in Ontario, he aspired to be the education premier, not just in name but in a deep "all systems go" manner. He studied Britain's reform strategy, asked me to join him, and got elected as premier in Ontario in October, 2003. Over the past six years (including a large majority reelection in 2007), Dalton did not lose the plot. He thickened it to the point that Ontario now has one of the most explicit whole-system models around. McGuinty remains, for me, the best self-conscious, deliberate, whole-system education reform leader in government anywhere in the world. I am biased, of course, but his strategy and its results are there for anyone to see—and we will take these up in the course of this book.

At the same time, we have the international benchmark stars as assessed by the Organization for Economic Cooperation and Development's (OECD) Program for International Student Assessment (PISA) with its highly regarded testing of the performance of 15-year-olds in literacy, science, and math—the top performers are Finland, Hong Kong, Singapore, South Korea, and Canada (Ontario and Alberta; PISA includes all Canadian provinces and reports results separately for each—there is no federal presence in education government in Canada). The first three are smallish (5 million people or so) and not diverse in the same way as the United States and Canada. Korea is large, but again not diverse; and because of its culture, it is able to pursue reform with a degree of resoluteness and top-downness.

We have something to learn from these high performers as I will identify in the book, but they are (except for Canada) too different to serve as models for whole-system reform in North America as a whole. Canada, for example, is more instructive for the United States, although it differs in some important respects. Alberta has led the way for many years with its collaborative alliances among the trustees association, superintendents, unions, and the government, although I don't feature their strategies in this book. Ben Levin, Ken Leithwood, and I are currently working with the College of Alberta School Superintendents and the Alberta Department of Education on their next wave of reform through, among other things, a major initiative on "Moving and Improving" school districts. It is Ontario that I feature in this book because it has a more explicit whole-system-reform approach that we will see reflected in the course of the various chapters.

And now, we have the new Obama administration with its highly touted Secretary of Education, Arne Duncan, and state governors around the United States who are trying to figure out how they slipped from number one in the world in high school and university attainment. For most of the 20th century (until about 1980) the United States led the world only to have its fortunes reversed with a steady decline in PISA parlance to about 24th. They are badly in need of making all systems go in the other direction.

There is quite a lot of focus in this book on improving education in the United States. This is partly because it represents such a large, egregious example of failed reform. In 1980, it had one of the most accomplished public education systems in the world. Over the past 30 years, it has slipped while other countries have steadily passed it. All this while *quadrupling* its education expenditure (see Grubb, 2009; Hanushek & Lindseth, 2009). How fascinating! (A phrase I borrowed from Michael Barber [2008] who used it for a different situation.)

The reason for paying attention now to the United States is that there appears to be a growing awareness in that country about the need to really do something about its slipping performance. Another fascination—when the first cracks were already in evidence, a national commission report dramatically concluded in 1983, "if an unfriendly foreign power had attempted to impose on America the mediocre educational performance that exists today, we might well have viewed it as an act of war" (National Commission on Excellence in Education, 1983). As things got worse, from there on in it seemed the giant could not waken itself. External forces in the form of at least 20 countries evidently and transparently outperforming the United States in a globally interdependent world might be the wake up call that works. The emphasis on the United States notwithstanding, this book also draws on policies and strategies of other successful countries, including Canada, Asia, and Scandinavian jurisdictions.

This book tackles whole-system reform in a practical way based on our experience and the evidence. I boil it down to a small number of critical components while advising that the "distractors"— strategies that waste time and resources and clutter the problem—be stripped away. I have written equally for politicians and professionals, whatever level they are at—local, intermediate, or system— teachers, principals, community leaders, superintendents, board members, state department officials, state commissioners, governors, premiers, presidents. All systems go must encompass all leaders. In a companion book to this one (Fullan, 2010, and forthcoming), I have captured the solution as a motion-leadership proposition. *Motion Leadership: The Skinny on Becoming Change Savvy* addresses what leaders do to get positive movement forward by using the smallest number of powerful, high-leverage strategies that any leader with effort can master. *All Systems Go* is the skinny on getting whole-system reform—any politician can do this with focus and effort.

In Part I, I take an overview look at the system as a whole. In Chapter 1, the basic idea of whole-system reform is addressed, including what it looks like and why it is critical to the success of any country, indeed the world. In Chapter 2, I show why most current strategies are bound to fail. They look good from a distance; but upon closer inspection, they are a gross waste of political, human, and fiscal resources. They badly fail the collective-capacity test.

The three chapters in Part II take up the details of whole-system reform at the school, district, and state levels—what it really looks like and ideas for getting there. It is in these chapters that I make the critical distinction between collective capacity (which is exponentially powerful) and individual capacity (which is necessary but not sufficient).

In Part III, Chapter 6, I focus on the most difficult and decidedly essential part of the solution—how politicians and professionals must unite, maintaining their respective roles and responsibilities for their own good and for the good of society as a whole. If we can get this right, we will enter a new era in which whole-system reform will become a continuous reality.

We now know enough to make all systems go. It will be difficult but is definitely doable. If there is one domain in society where everyone wins, it is by increasing the educational attainment of all students. It is time to raise the bar and reduce the gap for all citizens. We have never come as close to knowing how to do this as we are now. It is complex work but, as we shall see, not the least bit mysterious.

Acknowledgments

When it comes to thinking about and doing whole-system reform, I have three heroes whom I will introduce chronologically, according to the time I encountered them. I first worked with Sir Michael Barber in 1997, his first year as chief architect of Tony Blair's nationwide literacy and numeracy strategy (LNS) in England. We bid on and won the contract to evaluate LNS, which we did from 1998 to 2002. Sir Michael has been a close friend and colleague ever since, as he helped us in the Ontario reform, and in his current work as global-education-system transformer. No one knows about system reform in as many countries around the world as Michael. His book, *Instruction to Deliver* (2008), is one of the finest and most engaging accounts concerning inside the government politics and action.

Ben Levin came along shortly after as a member of our education team on LNS, but it was when we intercepted him on his way to the Ontario Institute for Studies in Education (OISE)/University of Toronto in 2004 that I really got to know him as Deputy Minister appointed to lead the civil service in our new Ontario reform (a job that he took a second time in 2009, when we needed him). No one moves in and out from government to academia with such consummate ease as Ben (except that his blood pressure goes up and down—guess which job is more taxing). Ben's book, *How to Change 5000 Schools* (2008) is also a gem.

The third wise man from whom I have learned a great deal is Premier Dalton McGuinty. In 2002, when he was leader of the opposition in Ontario with an eye to the 2003 election, he visited England to see what he could learn from their education-reform strategy. He knew that Tony Blair had made "education, education, education" his mantra and he wanted to do him one better. Michael Barber and his colleagues advised McGuinty to come and see me; my office was a few blocks from his back in Toronto, although we had never met. We got together along with his chief adviser, Gerald Butts, and I gave them a copy of my book, *The New Meaning of Educational Change* (now in its 4th edition, 2007). Three days later, they called me and said, "This is the agenda we want." Dalton and his crew, with my help, created Ontario's reform strategy. When he got elected in October, 2003, he appointed me as his special adviser in education. We then proceeded to formulate and implement a whole-system-reform strategy that we have been pursuing ever since, including building on a renewed mandate from the public via a large majority second term in 2007. No one combines politics, heart, and change savvy like Dalton. He too would write a great book if he had the time. No one knows how to make whole systems go like Premier McGuinty. Beyond the Premier, Ministers of Education Gerard Kennedy and Kathleen Wynne have been fabulous forces for rapport with teachers, parents, and communities. Rarely does one get to work with politicians who have both the moral commitment and the strategic know how to enact widespread successful reform.

Thus, I have learned and continue to learn so much from these leaders of system reform. Quite literally, this book could not have been written without their wise and sustained "thinking and doing."

The next set of heroes consists of the scores of teachers, principals, superintendents, state officials, and other officials whom I have worked with, especially since 1997 when the whole-system-reform agenda started in earnest. When I began my career as a know-nothing assistant professor in 1968, I brought theory to the table. Broadly, it helped me to at least fix on implementation and the meaning of educational change. Growingly, and in the past 10 years exponentially, the tables have been reversed. Nowadays, I learn from practice. Practice to theory improves theory because it operationalizes it in specific causal terms. With this tight nexus between practice and theory, you can be more precise and clear using fewer words to capture complex phenomena, something I call "motion leadership: the skinny on becoming change savvy" (Fullan, 2010).

My sincere thanks to Peter Senge for doing the foreword. If anyone has been the voice for system thinking and system reform for the past quarter of a century it has been Peter. It is an honor to have him associated with this book.

My publisher, Corwin, and its senior editor, Arnis Burvikovs; production editor, Cassandra Seibel; and copy editor, Adam Dunham, are godsends to work with—flexible, creative, contributing, high quality input from start to finish. I thank them for their commitment to quality. As always, deep thanks to Claudia Cuttress for her initiative and management of the variety of endeavors we always seem to have underway, including this one. It's great to have a manager that combines creativity, quality, and speed. And to Wendy for making all systems go, all the time on the home front. Overall, I am blessed with the incredible opportunity to do meaningful work supported by a myriad of others.

About the Author

 **Michael Fullan** is professor emeritus at the Ontario Institute for Studies in Education at the University of Toronto and is special adviser on education to Dalton McGuinty, the premier of Ontario. He holds honorary doctorates from the University of Edinburgh, Scotland, and from Nipissing University in Canada.

Fullan served as dean of the faculty of education at the University of Toronto from 1988 to 2003, leading two major organizational transformations, including a merger of two large schools of education. He is currently working as adviser and consultant on several major education reform initiatives around the world.

He bases his work on research and practice on both the public and private sectors, finding an increasing convergence in this literature. He has written several bestsellers on leadership and change that have been translated into several languages. Four of his books have won book-of-the-year awards. His latest books are *The Six Secrets of Change, Realization* (with Lyn Sharratt), and *Motion Leadership: The Skinny on Becoming Change Savvy.*

To Vince, wise beyond his schooling

PART I

The System

CHAPTER ONE

The Idea and Importance of Whole-System Reform

In this chapter, I sketch the idea of what whole-system reform looks like and then take up the question of why it is so vital to the future of societies. More detail comes in later chapters. *All systems go* means that every vital part of the whole system—school, community, district, and government contributes individually and in concert to forward movement and success. When it works, and I am talking practically, amazing things get accomplished with less effort; or more accurately, wasted effort gives way to energizing action. Above all, this book is focused on what realistically can be done.

There is nothing in the proposed solutions that we and others have not already done in practice. It is true that politicians tend to go for superficial bullets. The actual solutions, however, are not that much more complicated, but they do require relentless focus on a small number of key interrelated policies and strategies. My purpose in *All Systems Go* is to capture the set of interrelated strategies that work.

There are some "big ideas" in this book and I should highlight them in advance (see Exhibit 1.1).

Exhibit 1.1	Big Ideas for Whole-System Reform

1. All children can learn
2. A small number of key priorities
3. Resolute leadership/stay on message
4. Collective capacity
5. Strategies with precision
6. Intelligent accountability
7. All means all

Of course, many say that all children can learn, failure is not an option (except that evidently it is), and so on. The big idea in this book is that they really can learn, and all systems go proves that it can be done. All children (95%), except the severely disabled, can learn to a high level of critical reasoning and problem solving. And those who are seriously disadvantaged (physically or mentally) can lead effective lives through inclusionary developmentally based programs typical of all-systems-go reforms.

Second, every successful organization pursues a small number of core priorities (that have leverage power) and does them exceedingly well. We include literacy and numeracy—not the narrow testing of No Child Left Behind, but also higher-order thinking, reasoning and problem-solving skills—and we link them to whole-child development, emotional well-being, music, dance, and the arts. And we pursue high-quality literacy and numeracy into high schools and related higher education and career choices.

Third, we are beginning to appreciate that successful schools, districts, and larger systems have "resolute leadership" that stays with the focus, especially during rough periods, and these leaders cause others around them to be resolute. It is so easy to go off message, and if you do, you lose whole-system-reform possibilities. This is hard, persistent work but it is not overly complex. Resolute leadership is critical near the beginning when new ideas encounter serious difficulty, but it is also required to sustain and build on success.

Fourth, another big idea that is not new but is very much underappreciated is that *collective capacity* is the hidden resource we fail to understand and cultivate. As Morten Hansen (2009) says, collaboration is not an end in itself. The question is what is the difference between good and bad collaboration, and when are certain kinds of collaboration worse than no collaboration. Hansen calls for "disciplined collaboration," which my term covers in the use of the word *capacity*. We will return to Hansen in Chapter 2. In the meantime, you cannot get whole-system reform without counting on collective (as distinct from individual) capacity, and this book is full of concrete examples of this in action. Incidentally, as I will explain later, we have discovered the intriguing phenomenon of "collaborative competition" whereby you simultaneously benefit from both collaboration and competition (Boyle, 2009).

Strategies with precision is another core idea of *All Systems Go*. I will furnish numerous examples of specificity and precision in particular strategies. When you have precision, as I will show, the *speed of quality change* can be greatly accelerated. Incredible and convincing transformations can be accomplished in schools in one short year through precision strategies.

Sixth, the failure to get accountability right plagues all reform efforts. All systems go has figured it out through the concept of *intelligent accountability*. Andy Hargreaves unlocked this door when he observed that "accountability is the remainder that is left when . . . responsibility has been subtracted" (Hargreaves & Shirley, 2009, p. 102). Intelligent accountability involves a set of policies and practices that actually increases individual, and especially collective, capacity to the transparent point that shared responsibility carries most of the freight of effective accountability; that makes internal and external accountability almost seamless; and that leaves external accountability to do its remaining, more-manageable task of necessary intervention.

Finally, *all* really does mean *all*. You can't solve the problem of whole-system reform through piecemeal efforts that try to get parts of the system improving in order to show the way. System reform does not, cannot work that way—a critique I take up in Chapter 2.

THE IDEA OF WHOLE-SYSTEM REFORM

The School and the Community

Grade-2 teacher Irina Fedra just finished a shared reading exercise with a small group that included two Somali boys and a girl who had arrived at the school 6 months earlier not speaking a word of English. They can actually read, thought Irina. By next year at the end of Grade 3, they will probably meet the province's high standard assessment in reading and writing.

Of her 15 years of teaching, Irina has learned more about quality instruction in the past 3 years than in the previous 12 years combined. Quality instruction requires getting a small number of practices right. These practices involve knowing clearly and specifically what each student can or cannot do, followed by tailored intervention that engages students in the particular learning in question, and then doing the assessment-instruction-correction process on a continuous basis. This is decidedly not drill and test. In our work in literacy and numeracy in Ontario, the instruction goals include higher-order reasoning, problem solving, and expression, with the associated practices becoming more and more specific and precise.

In systems that go, strategies focus on and drill down to effective instructional practices so that *all* teachers, individually and collectively, become better at what they are doing while they continue to seek even better methods. This is the domain of expertise that John Hattie (2009) is getting at in his synthesis of over 800 meta-analyses of teaching practices related to student engagement and achievement. High-impact strategies such as structured feedback to students, reciprocal teaching (teaching students to learn cognitive strategies to facilitate their own learning), and observation and feedback on ones' own teaching all had high impact on student learning. Hattie tells us that the critical change agents are

- Knowledge and skills
- A plan of action
- Strategies to overcome setbacks
- A high sense of confidence
- Monitoring progress
- A commitment to achieve
- Social and environment support
- Freedom, control, or choice

Irina is learning to become a professional exactly along the lines that Hattie is talking about—engaging in specific, precise, evidence-based, high-yield instructional practices. She is learning this because she is part of a comprehensive *collective-capacity* enterprise. Within the school, she learns from other teachers, the literacy coach, and the principal (and contributes to their learning). They have "data walls" for their use only, where she sees the individual progress for each of her 20 students, and that of the other 40 students in the other two Grade-2 classes. She meets with the team, including the principal who participates as a learner and leader in assessing samples of student work, in order to identify corrective action.

Irina gets a chance to practice new instructional methods with feedback from the literacy coach. She is a member of the school-leadership team that participates in capacity-building sessions with other schools in the district. The school has access to instructional materials, short video clips demonstrating specific instructional techniques, and cross visitations to other schools farther down the track.

Irina is also part of a buddy-day strategy in her school that the district and her principal introduced. Although it started on a small scale, buddy days are now once a month. Every grade-level primary teacher (Grades 1–3) is buddied with a teacher at the junior level (Grades 4–6). The two buddied teachers plan the buddy-day monthly activities together. This allows the teachers to plan a two-day activity. One day, the junior teacher would be supervising the whole group; the next day the primary teacher would be overseeing the group as they complete the activity. Older children have the opportunity to explain and lead the activity with their younger buddies. The buddy days focus on literacy and math. The activities developed are kept in a binder for wider sharing and reference about hands-on teaching with mixed age groupings. All activities are assessed in terms of their impact on student engagement and learning. The principal participates as a learner in all sessions, as part of working with teachers in a collaborative way in order to focus the school on high-yield strategies. The we-we commitment that gets generated among the children and the teachers is enormous. The sense of allegiance to one's peers and to the school as a whole that gets generated by these purposeful collaborations is palpable. Collective pride and desire to do better is evident everywhere.

All of this works. Irina's school has gone from 33% of its students scoring high proficiency on the province's annual assessment of literacy to 82% in three years! As the principal and teachers experienced initial success (one could say as they began to know what they were doing), they began to involve parents and the community. She is involved in the school's multifaceted efforts that include parent/family town hall sessions, street festivals, heritage and English language classes, food nights, extensive use of the school facilities including the library. Irina and her colleagues also have a keen interest in participating in the province's new "early-learning initiative," which includes health, nutrition, and other care for preschoolers (nine months to three years of age), full-day service for all four- and five-year-olds, and extended day for all children preschool to eight-years-old.

Albert Quah is a student success teacher (SST) in a diversely populated high school of 1,300 students. His job is to help kids who might be on the verge of failing or dropping out to reengage in their education, and to connect to those who recently left to see if he can get them back in school. He knows the literature that says that often the difference between staying or going for many borderline students is whether they have a meaningful relationship with one or more caring adults. He also knows that it is not just a matter of caring, but whether these students, many of them bright, have something meaningful at school that interests them. Thus, Albert must care, but he also must help to make program innovations.

Albert and his colleagues have done the following things. The province has a Grade-10 mandatory literacy test called the Ontario Secondary School Literacy Test (OSSLT), which students must pass to graduate from high school. He and the instructionally oriented principal and leadership team lead the blitzing of OSSLT preparation. The whole school is involved in after-school programs for small groups of students who need help; within-school small classes for certain groups, and the highly successful PLANT (peer literacy and numeracy tutoring) initiative in which Grade-11 and -12 students are trained to work with Grade-9 and -10 students. The program is a huge success in which both tutors and tutees learn (to the point where several of the tutors get so turned on that they plan to become future teachers).

Albert and his colleagues also run "rescue and recovery" courses for students who are letting certain courses sink. Students must earn a certain number of credits in order to receive a high school diploma. If they get behind in credits in Grades 9 and 10, most never catch up. Through analyzing the data on individual student profiles, the school discovered that as many as 25% of the students were falling behind. Knowing which students in which subjects were failing, Albert's job as SST is to work specifically on helping students do something about it. They use two innovations—"credit rescue" and "credit recovery." Credit rescue comes into play before the student has actually failed the course. Working with the particular teachers, faltering students are identified partway through the course and interventions are made that increase the student's chance of passing the course—activities such as help with personal problems, tutoring, classroom assistance, e-learning, and so on.

Credit recovery takes place after a student has failed a course. The credit recovery team, chaired by one of the most respected science teachers, approves each case. In many cases, students who failed did well on 40% or so of the material. Once a student is approved, a course is designed that has the student working on only those course requirements in which he or she has been unsuccessful. The course is designed specifically for the individual student and must meet the rigor of all other courses. The evaluation process includes course work and a culminating activity.

Albert and his student-success coordinator at the district office have taken the credit accumulation question one step further. Why wait until a student is in need of rescue or recovery? Instead, they have begun to identify those students, by name, coming from their feeder schools into Grade 9, who might be at risk. They know these names in August, before the school year has begun, and they provide targeted support related to both personal and schooling issues where needed. They don't even have a name for this initiative (credit anticipation?). They know what all successful systems know—intervene early and as often as necessary.

Another more radical and highly successful program innovation is called the high skills major (HSM). New specialties are created for students who find the abstract academic program not to their liking. They have little interest in and are not good at abstract thinking just for the sake of it. Normally, such students get increasingly alienated, drop out, or get streamed to dead-end technical courses. HSM is not just for nonacademic students; many "academic students" are also in the program. This is what sets HSM apart from traditional (and dead-end) vocational programs. The idea is to combine intellectual and practical work in various ways for all students. (As an aside, many so-called academic courses are not all that theoretical or intellectual anyway; good theory must be grounded in practice, and vice-versa).

The HSM programs allows schools and districts to work with employers and community groups to create packages of courses leading to employment and further learning. Albert knows that HSMs have been created in other schools in areas such as mining, tourism, agriculture, and manufacturing, which include links to colleges for further postsecondary learning and credentials. Albert, given the interests of some of his students, proposes and gets approval to offer an HSM in transportation. One of the girls, alienated from most of her courses, becomes interested. It turns out that she and her father race cars on the weekend, and she knows a great deal about engines. Early in the course, she asks her teacher if it would be okay if her father brought their racecar to school. Two weeks later, a flatbed truck pulls into the parking lot with a gleaming racecar that looks like it has been plucked from the Formula 1 Grand Prix circuit. That girl is now reengaged! And doing well in her other courses to boot.

Albert is reminded of a book he just read, *Shop Class as Soul Craft* (Crawford, 2009). The author shows that hands-on technical work is every bit as cognitive as any academic endeavor. Crawford has a PhD in philosophy, and a love for motorcycles, especially fixing them. The motorcycles win out as a career choice. Albert has some of Crawford's observations on his office wall—"I often find manual work more engaging *intellectually*"; "Creativity is a by-product of the mastery of the sort that is cultivated through long practice"; and "The truth does not reveal itself to idle spectators." Had Albert read more widely, he would have found kindred spirits in Henry Mintzberg (2004), who argues that abstract thinking is not even good thinking, and makes you a dangerous doer; or how about the Hopper brothers (2009), who lay the blame for the deterioration of business and industry on the shift from applied to abstract management starting around 1970—almost the same period, as we saw earlier, wherein America commenced its educational decline. The right kind of doing is grounded intellectualism and that is the business that Albert and his colleagues are in.

HSM is one of those elegant innovations that does not require major structural change and does not cost very much, as it draws on the collective resources of partners that already exist. The program began only in 2006/2007 with 600 students. Now in its fourth year, more than 20,000 students are enrolled in 740 HSM programs in 430 schools involving 70 of the 72 school districts in Ontario. These programs are connected to 16 industrial sectors. This is truly an example of spontaneous collective-capacity development that hardly cost the system anything.

Back to Albert. In addition to the HSM program at his school that serves students in Grades 11 and 12, Albert is monitoring the progress of Grade-9 and -10 students, especially with respect to literacy. The targeted efforts are getting results. The percentage of students passing the OSSLT—the province's mandatory literacy assessment—has gone from 65 to 81. The high school graduation rate has also moved upward, beating the provincial average that is itself climbing.

Like Irina, Albert's work is successful because it is nested in school, district, and state strategies that are interrelated for this purpose. There are 972 student success teachers in the province (one per school and a coordinating SST for each district). Paid for by the state but employed by the district, SSTs focus on direct student advocacy and mentoring and school-wide staff development. The SSTs communicate with staff and parents and work with subject-specific teachers in meeting the needs of students who are struggling.

The SSTs work in their schools and districts, and they also learn from each other. The SST coordinator at the district level selects, trains, and networks the 14 SSTs (there are 14 high schools in Albert's district). The coordinators also arrange for cross-site visits to other districts in their region. And the head of the program at the state level's Ministry of Education conducts regional and once-a-year provincewide sessions of SSTs to exchange ideas and address issues as well as keeps in touch throughout the year.

It seems to be working in that the high school graduation rate in the province has steadily increased from 68% to 77% in its 900 schools over the past four years. Albert knows that 14,000 more students are graduating from high school each year in the province compared to four years ago, and that he is contributing to that number. And Albert knows that most of the better, more-focused innovations have not yet had a chance to have their full impact. This interrelated set of high school innovations has plenty of yield left in it. Albert is pretty confident that the initial provincial target of 85% high school graduation will be met within the next three years.

In brief, Irina and Albert are great teachers and change agents. But what makes them most effective is that they are not alone—connection, coherence, and collective-capacity building characterize the entire system from classroom to school to district to state.

District Level

Irina's and Albert's schools are successful because they are nested in a district that is running on a focused, coherent all-systems-go mode (see Chapter 3 for a fuller characterization). District leadership has its act together. No silos of standards, curriculum and instruction, personnel, finance, and so on. No we-they mentality between the districts and the schools or across schools but rather vibrant two-way and multiway partnerships zeroing in on instruction and results. In Chapter 2, we will see specific examples of named districts operating in this mode in Canada, England, and the United States.

Irina and Albert's districts use one of the most powerful strategies we know of in order to get whole-district reform, namely *lateral capacity building.* Schools are in small clusters with a coordinating supervisor. They learn from each other in an ongoing, purposeful way. Beyond the clusters, schools learn from other schools in the district. They celebrate results and identify what's working or not. They develop a fierce sense of pride and "collaborative competition" (see Boyle, 2009, and Fullan, 2010) in what they learn from each other as they try to outdo one another—for the challenge of it, for the good of the higher moral purpose (raise the bar and close the gap for all).

In the partnership, the district presses forward; it is responsive to schools; it fosters transparency of results and of practice; it provides good and timely data on how schools are faring; it intervenes in a nonpunitive manner in schools that are struggling. Irina and Albert's district also integrate individual and collective capacity. With respect to the former, personnel policies and practices are aligned with the instructional focus in the hiring and development of teachers, selection and cultivation of leaders (literacy and numeracy coaches, student-success teachers—part of the high school strategy), potential future school leaders, beginning and continuing assistant principals, and principals.

Their district, or rather the whole set of schools in the district, also enjoys success (not all smooth or linear) as literacy and numeracy increases across the board, Grade-9 math and literacy get better, and high school graduation dramatically rises.

State Level

The district too is nested in a larger system of districts that make up the public school system of Ontario. There are 13 million people in Ontario, 2 million students, 4,000 elementary and 900 secondary schools in 72 districts (see Chapter 4).

The same phenomenon of collective-capacity development that occurs within Irina's and Albert's schools, and within their districts' schools, is at work in the public school system as a whole. The change principles are identical, albeit at a more complex level.

First, the government had to get its act together, especially in relation to its ministry of education (state department). They did three things: (1) focused on a small number of ambitious instructional goals; (2) created an instructional capacity capability (which they did not initially have) to help lead the field in partnership—this involved a 100-person Literacy and Numeracy Secretariat, and a smaller student success (SS) group to work with high schools (the Literacy and Numeracy Secretariat and the SS group are now integrated); (3) worked on changing the culture of the ministry so that it had greater internal coherence and a commitment to work in a two-way partnership with the 4,900 schools and the 72 districts.

Some districts were ahead of the government when the new strategies began in 2003 (making for a great resource for others), but many were not being successful. The strategy in question is an all-systems-go proposition, and thus the goal is to engage *the whole system* in a coherent focused effort.

There is no getting around it. For the entire system to be on the move, you need relentless, resolute leadership from the top— leadership that focuses on the right things and that above all promotes collective capacity and ownership. The top needs to do a small number of critical things well: establish high expectations and ambitious but achievable targets, for example, in literacy, numeracy, and high school graduation rates—targets that are negotiable within the subunits of districts and schools; form a partnership with the field (the education sector); increase its capacity to contribute to the partnership; invest in capacity building by helping to identify and spread good practice; intervene in a nonpunitive manner in situations that need improvement; engage in constant, transparent communication about results and next steps; and buttress the central-focused strategies with mid- to long-term reinforcements such as early learning for preschool children; teacher recruitment and development; and school and district leadership cultivation, support, and development. And the top needs to attend carefully to all core relationships—the public, parents, teacher unions, and senior elements of the education sector itself.

Some examples: Ontario has a turnaround schools strategy called OFIP (Ontario Focused Intervention Partnership) that addresses those schools and districts that are low performing or coasting (average but flat-lined in performance). It is an expansive program involving some 1,000 of the 4,000 elementary schools in total. Nonpunitive but explicit in nature, OFIP provides direct capacity-building experiences relative to literacy and numeracy using a precise "critical learning pathways" model suited to the school. In most cases, positive results occur within two months, to be built on by the district and the Literacy and Numeracy Secretariat together. OFIP schools gain on the average 10% more in student achievement than do other schools (see Chapter 4).

Another example is the "Schools on the Move" strategy in which some 150 schools have been identified on the basis of having achieved significant improvement for three straight years on at least four of the six main measures (Grade-3 reading, writing, and math, and Grade-6 reading, writing, and math). These schools are profiled publicly with respect to their demographics, achievement scores, and strategies used. They are given money so that other schools can learn from them, not as in "why can't you be more like your brother," but rather in the spirit that this is hard work, some are making more progress than others, what can we learn from them?

There are other similar strategies making the system go through mechanisms of learning from each other and firm but nonpunitive accountability. All in all, you have just seen a snapshot of what whole-system reform looks like. It is based on a true story, in this case in Ontario. Not that the province has arrived, but everything I described above exists (except for the names of Irina Fedra and Albert Quah). Ubiquitous increases in instructional capacity are required—in every classroom, every school, and every district. Yes, individual capacity is part of the development, but at the end of the day *only collective capacity counts*, if you want whole-system reform. The pressure and support of two-way partnerships across and within each of the three levels of schools and communities, districts, and states are required. Coordination, focus, easy access to best ideas, the press of collaborative competition and ultimately win-win outcomes are the drivers. There is simply and flatly no other way to get whole-system reform. We are not talking about a few good schools here and there. All 4,900 schools are engaged in the reform.

THE IMPORTANCE OF WHOLE-SYSTEM REFORM

The Big Picture

Of course, an increase in the average level of educational achievement in a society is important, but light years better is whether the gap between high and low achievers decreases as the overall average rises. Closing the gap has profound multiple benefits for both individuals and for society as a whole. Large gaps spell doom. The facts are impressive and scary.

Andreas Schleicher (2009a) is the head of the Indicators and Analysis division of OECD. He runs PISA. In the 1960s, the United States was number one in the world in terms of the percentage of adults with high school qualifications (87%); by the 1990s, they were 13th. In 1995, the United States was number one in post-secondary graduation rates and they spent the most money per student. By 2005, they still spent the most money per student, but by that time they were surpassed by Australia and 12 other countries.

The PISA assessments themselves are based on large samples of 15-year-olds who are tested in literacy, math, and science not on a narrow base of knowledge but rather "looking ahead to how well they can extrapolate from what they have learned and apply their knowledge and skills in novel settings" (Schleicher, 2009a). For example, in science, PISA measures knowledge (knowledge of and about science), and science competencies (ability to identify, explain, and use scientific evidence).

The more telling result is whether a country is able to get both high average test scores (in science, math, and literacy) and have low income-based inequality (what PISA calls "social equity" [Schleicher, 2009a; 2009b], relative to other countries. To use the United States as reference point, there are 18 countries that have surpassed them in literacy, math, and science over the last 30 years (Finland, Canada, Sweden, Australia, South Korea, etc., etc.).

In further analysis of the economic impact of the achievement gap, Michael Barber and his colleagues at McKinsey (McKinsey & Co., 2009) conclude that "these education gaps impose on the United States the economic equivalent of a *permanent national recession*" (p. 5, emphasis in original). McKinsey & Co. calculates that, had the United States closed the education achievement gap to levels comparable to Finland and Korea, the impact on GDP would be 1.3 to 2.3 trillion higher (a 9%–16% increase); if the gap between black and Latino student performance and white student performance was similarly narrowed, the GDP would have been 310 to 525 billion higher; if the gap between low-income and high-income students were narrowed, the contribution to the GDP would be 400 to 670 billion higher. And so on.

The Alliance for Excellent Education (2008) draws a similar conclusion in their report "Dropouts, Diplomas, and Dollars." As the Alliance reports, for every 100 ninth-grade students, only 40 enroll in college, only 27 are still enrolled in their sophomore year, and only 18 graduate from college or university. The figures are worse for Hispanics and Blacks. The costs to individuals and society are enormous. The dropouts themselves suffer the most direct impact. Society also suffers. If the students who dropped out in 2008 had actually graduated, the nation would have benefited from an additional $319 billion in income over their lifetimes, not to mention savings in health costs, prisons, and the like (p. 2).

The Even Bigger Picture

We have already seen that the United States spends much more per pupil on education than any other country, *and* they have one of the most unequal distributions of education attainment, with large gaps between high and low performers, *and* countries with lower gaps have better literacy, science, and math scores. Let's cut quickly to the biggest picture. Richard Wilkinson and Kate Pickett (2009)—just considering the richest countries in the world (i.e., the OECD group)—document in compelling detail "why more equal societies almost always do better." We can just take one of over a dozen similar graphs presented by Wilkinson and Pickett. Exhibit 1.2 displays the relationship between income inequality and an index of health and social problems.

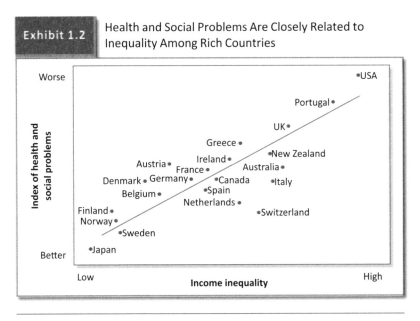

Exhibit 1.2 Health and Social Problems Are Closely Related to Inequality Among Rich Countries

Source: Wilkinson & Pickett, 2009, p. 20.

Income inequality (remember the comparison involves only the richest countries in the world) is associated with lower levels of trust, more mental illness, lower life expectancy, obesity, children's educational performance, teenage births, homicides, imprisonment rates, and so on. It is true that the rich are better off than the poor in all societies, but by comparison across societies, whether rich or poor, you do worse in an unequal society. Wilkinson and Pickett show this to be the case for diabetes, hypertension, cancer, and lung and heart disease (p. 192). As one further illustration, the death rates in the lowest classes in Sweden (the more equal society) are lower than the death rates in the highest class in England and Wales (the less equal society).

Let's leave aside the moral argument that higher percentages of poor people in an unequal rich society live lives of misery and die earlier, and let's just consider the societal costs. Unequal rich societies face greater costs on just about every dimension that counts: health, delinquency, incarceration, death, violence, social cohesion, civic engagement (including voting), and of course economic losses in the billions. All of this is compounded in light of the fact that many other countries are on the move to greater equality and prosperity in a globally competitive world.

CONCLUSION

We saw a glimpse of whole-system reform in the first half of this chapter. It involves *all* schools in the system getting better, including reducing the gap between high and low performers. Whole-system reform produces higher levels of education performance on important cognitive and social learning goals, and it does so while reducing the gap toward a more equal public education system. I did not feature the United States in whole-system reform examples in this chapter because there are no examples of whole states achieving this level of coherence and focus. (There are isolated districts that have accomplished systemwide reform—these are taken up in Chapter 3—and Darling-Hammond [2010] has found that some states have been on the right track for short periods of time.)

We also saw why whole-system reform matters so much, both in direct terms and in almost all aspects of societal functioning. Of course, there is a tricky chicken-and-egg relationship between unequal income distribution and unequal education attainment in a society. Later on, I will acknowledge the need for non-school policies and strategies to address inequality, but this book is primarily about what the education sector can contribute to reducing inequality. The answer is that a great deal can be done, and we know how to do it. In fact, it is possible with focused effort that effective schools and systems can virtually eliminate the role of socioeconomic status (SES) in determining educational attainment. The correlation between SES and education success can at least be greatly reduced if not eliminated altogether. But first, we need to address what not to do—mainly because it wastes valuable resources while the clock continues to tick downward.

C H A P T E R   T W O

Deceptive Inadequacies

There are three critical clarifications to make before we launch into this and subsequent chapters: (1) the nature of the core skills required, (2) a conceptualization of the term *resources*, and (3) the components of successful whole-school reform.

First, the emphasis needs to be on *higher order skills* for everyone in the system. People sometimes make the mistake of thinking that reading the words on the page is literacy or that being able to add and subtract is numeracy. And others rightly criticize the folly of just focusing on narrow testing (Rothstein, Jacobsen, and Wilder, 2008). Rather than throwing out literacy and numeracy, it is better to recast them (as we have done) into their more fundamental and lateral-leverage role in fostering whole-child development. The whole-system reform goals that we are considering in this book are more than the basics. They also evolve easily into the 21st-century skills, and have the virtue of forcing greater specificity relative to 21st-century–skills assessment and corresponding instruction.

The Ontario assessment system, for example, focuses on reading, writing, and mathematics. It considers reasoning, problem solving, critical analysis, and so forth. OECD's PISA assessments do not just focus on what students have learned but also on "how well they can extrapolate what they have learned and apply their knowledge and skills in novel settings." (Schleicher, 2009a, p. 2). OECD is moving towards assessing collaborative problem solving and digital literacy, including electronic delivery for all assessment domains. If you just take basic reading, Ontario has an achievement rate of over 90%. If you add the more demanding higher-order skills, only about 2/3 of the students are operating at this level.

In the same vein, CISCO, Intel, and Microsoft have teamed up to fund a development initiative on "Assessing and Teaching 21st Century Skills" (Cisco, Intel, & Microsoft, 2009) in which they have contracted top academics to develop "assessments and instructional practices" with respect to eight 21st-century skills (creativity, problem solving, critical thinking, collaboration, and so on). They rightly say that (1) these skills are critical, (2) good assessments of them do not exist, and (3) the corresponding instructional practices to teach them have not been developed (see also Trilling and Fadel, 2009).

My point is that when we advocate a small number of ambitious instructional priorities we include this movement towards the deeper skills and their application to functioning in dynamic societies of the future.

Second, I need to say a word about resources (let's call it *money plus*). Our solution to whole-system reform will require a more sophisticated (but never overly complex) conception of resources. Grubb (2009) offers the most useful set of definitions (he talks about four kinds of resources, but we need only the first three). He helps us by saying that there are *simple, compound,* and *complex* resources.

Simple resources pertain to single-factor investments. For example, a new policy calls for reduction in class size. Compound resources involve two factors, such as reduced class size plus professional development directed at teaching differently in the smaller classes. Complex resources refer to a combination of factors (three or more) that go together, such as reduced class size, professional learning, and the instructional leadership of a focused, collaborative principal.

These distinctions are crucial (remember we only get as complex as is practically necessary). Reducing class size requires very high expenditure; but if not linked with professional development, the impact is almost nil (see Whelan, 2009). When it comes to money, you can buy class size reduction, but you can't fully buy quality professional development or instructional leadership. For these complex resources, some money is required, but it is a resource that you literally cannot buy. You have to develop it on the ground. Whole-system reform is about focusing on fostering and use of complex resources. It is complex, but as we shall see, it is not a mystery.

Third, the main elements of successful whole-system reform coming from our experience and other evidence are contained in Exhibit 2.1. We use them in this chapter to show how current approaches to reform stack up against the criteria. Subsequent chapters flesh out the details of all systems go in action.

Exhibit 2.1   Elements of Successful Reform

1. A small number of ambitious goals

2. A guiding coalition at the top

3. High standards and expectations

4. Collective capacity building with a focus on instruction

5. Individual capacity building linked to instruction

6. Mobilizing the data as a strategy for improvement

7. Intervention in a nonpunitive manner

8. Being vigilant about "distractors"

9. Being transparent, relentless, and increasingly challenging

---

The details will come later, but the gist of this strategy is to mobilize and engage large numbers of people who are individually and collectively committed and effective at getting results relative to core outcomes that society values. It works because it is focused, relentless (stay the course), operates as a partnership between and across layers, and above all uses the collective energy of the whole group. There is no way of achieving whole-system reform if the vast majority of people are not working on it *together.*

Let's see how current and typical reform strategies measure up against this constellation of criteria for success.

Deceptive Inadequacies

It is not as if policymakers have not focused on systemwide reform. Ever since *A Nation At Risk* in 1983, reform wave after reform wave has been introduced culminating in recent times in the 2002 No Child Left Behind (NCLB) Act. Funding has quadrupled (even after adjusting for inflation). Adjusted to 2007, the spending growth from 1960 to 2005 rose from $2,606 per pupil to $9,910 (Hanushek & Lindseth, 2009, p. 45). In other words, school districts have four times the purchasing power today than they did 40 years ago. To take another number, from 1980 when decline began to be recognized and the call for system reform came loud and clear, the increase has been just under 70% in real dollars (from $5,900 to over $9,000).

So as to not take unfair examples, let's consider the highly touted (at the time of its passage) bipartisan No Child Left Behind Act. Hanushek and Lindseth (2009) report that endless policy, media stories, and public announcements begin and end with the words, "we must ensure that our children have the skills necessary to compete in the twenty-first century" (p. 10). What could be more whole system than that?

Like son, like father. President George H. W. Bush convened a meeting with the country's state governors in September, 1989. This summit meeting led to the adoption of six national education goals (later expanded to eight). Here are two: All children will start school ready to learn; United States students will be first in the world in mathematics and science achievement. They gave themselves until the year 2000 to accomplish this. No one seems to have noticed that 2000 came and went—except that it was time for another ambitious reform.

President George W. Bush, the son, launched the massive No Child Left Behind Act in 2001 (passed by Congress in 2002) that promised to have all groups of students in the country (Black, Latino, Asian, White, etc.) score at the proficient level by 2014 (and that there would be a qualified teacher in every classroom).

The fact that over both periods (1989–2009) the United States has steadily lost ground to other countries tells you that the strategies are dramatically wanting. Here are the most obvious problems:

- Pie-in-the-sky, unachievable goals;
- Too many goals and corresponding tests;
- NCLB mandates that every state sets standards, assesses them, and reports adequate yearly progress (AYP). The result is a dog's breakfast. A student in one state can score 70% on

the state reading test, while a comparable student in another state can score 50%; but in an objective third-party test, their results are reversed;

- There is virtually nothing in NCLB on capacity building—no means to get there;
- The timelines are too short, and they are punitive (increasingly bad things happen to you if you don't meet AYP); and
- As people jump through hoops, the whole thing has no meaning—and no credibility.

In short, it is impossible to expect any collective commitment and creativity to achieve the lofty goals vital to the future of the nation. NCLB has been valuable to highlight what the agenda should be, but it has not given advantage to the United States in any way relative to closing the gap within the country or to keeping pace on international comparators.

The waste of fiscal and human resources is appalling (recall that the United States keeps spending more and more). Norton Grubb (2009) gives us chapter and verse. He gives 10 types of examples:

1. Funds can be embezzled or spent to hire incompetent friends and relatives.

2. Funds can be spent on inputs that have no effect—textbooks, supplies, computers—as "single resources" that are not well used.

3. Resources can be used without changing practices, such as often happens following one-day professional-development workshops.

4. Funds can be spent on purely symbolic practices without accompanying capacity building.

5. Resources can be spent on well-intentioned-but-ineffective practices—*reform du jours*, Grubb calls them.

6. Funds can be spent on potentially good practices that are overturned when the principal or superintendent changes and comes in with his or her favorites.

7. Spending resources are piecemeal, which fails to get much-needed coherent change.

8. Resources may be spent on changes that are necessary but not sufficient, such as purchasing computers without providing teacher training.

9. All too often, principals do not know how to best use the resources they have.

10. Particularly in urban schools, a good deal of spending is on what Grubb calls "second chance efforts" (not getting something right in the first place), which represent extremely difficult circumstances for turning around cumulative disadvantages. (Grubb, 2009, pp. 29–31)

Grubb furnishes countless examples of wasted resources, concluding with these words:

For the most part . . . districts with higher expenditures per student invest them in single resources, ignoring a greater variety of effective practices. On the contrary, overall expenditures per pupil have had few and inconsistent effects on other resources, particularly those related to quality of instruction and to measures of school climate. While simple resources—such as additional teachers and increased salaries—can be bought, communities of educators must work together to construct most other resources. (p. 87)

My point is that, not only do existing strategies permit massive waste of resources on ineffective remedies, but they actually end up (unwittingly) fostering these very practices. They actually *cause* dysfunctional outcomes. As Grubb (2009) notes, NCLB has increased the pressure on schools to increase student performance quickly, and that pressure has driven many schools and districts "to adopt off-the-shelf programs that are of doubtful value and represent quick fixes in place of the longer-run process of enhancing teacher capacity and restructuring schools" (p. 249).

On the timeline with respect to our Exhibit 2.1 strategy, we can get significant results in a state or province within two years, and certainly within one election period. It can't be done overnight, but it can be done within one year, even in large schools. Precision strategies focusing on collective capacity dramatically accelerates the pace and effectiveness of change. Reform doesn't take a particularly long time to show positive results if the right combination of strategies is employed.

NCLB, as we have seen, has spawned much criticism. Eric Hanushek (an economist), and Alfred Lindseth (a lawyer) (2009) have teamed up to give us an incisive analysis of the problems, but come up with a defective solution. These authors corroborate Grubb's (2009) detailed analysis of the existing problem and huge waste of resources—"the problem is that we are not getting much return for our massive financial commitment" (p. 48).

Hanushek and Lindseth (2009) also treat us to a careful and frightening analysis of the history of cases pertaining to court intervention in school finance (only in America, you say). At the general level, at least 40 states have been taken to court over funding (with a little less than half of the settlements favoring the plaintiffs—i.e., cases where the state lost).

Courts understandably have not wanted to get into compound let alone complex resource strategies that our model calls for (too complicated for the court to monitor); so instead, they award money that is to be used to obtain greater equity. The most egregious award involved Kansas City, Missouri, School District (KCMSD). Relying on his authority to "desegregate" the district, Judge Russell Clark ordered over $2 billion in additional funds to be made available over the next twelve years to the district of 37,000 students. The district's annual budget ballooned from $125 million to $432 million; per-pupil funding became three times the amount of other districts in the state. Hundreds of millions of dollars were spent on state-of-the-art facilities, large across-the-board salary raises for all employees, reduced class size, thousands of computers, off-the-shelf programs for at-risk students, before- and after-school programs, the addition of thousands of new employees, and so on.

It won't surprise you to know that all this made no difference in student performance (Hanushek & Lindseth, 2009, p. 53). This example is dramatic but is only different in degree, not kind. The vast majority of court-awarded decisions to plaintiffs with corresponding new monies did not impact student learning because the strategy was simple minded—spend more money on piecemeal solutions.

Whether it is new money from NCLB, court orders, or whatever, you can't buy reform with simple resources, no matter how large. So what's the solution? Hanushek and Lindseth (2009) offer their version—carefully considered, but in my view inadequate to the task. It does not meet our Exhibit 2.1 criteria, and it will not in its own right produce the outcomes it seeks to determine.

Hanushek and Lindseth (2009) call their solution "a performance based funding system." Their model contains five big inter-related ideas:

1. Standards, assessment, and accountability;

2. Empower local decision making;

3. Direct rewards and incentives;

4. Information, evaluation, and continuous improvement; and

5. Rational and equitable funding. (adapted from Hanushek & Lindseth, 2009)

Although the model contains several elements that are compatible with Exhibit 2.1, the strategy as a whole will not and cannot result in the all-systems-go solution we are seeking. Overall, it would be a mammoth distractor, generating 10 years or more of debate about whether or not it can or should be implemented, not to mention the vagaries of implementation. It is too structural and too complicated for most people to comprehend and/or have faith in. I take up each of the five components briefly.

First, standards and assessment of challenging learning goals is necessary, and, in fact, a key part of my solution. But then, Hanushek and Lindseth (2009) begin to lose us. They say that policy should begin with "an explicit statement of the learning goals of schools—detailed by subject and grade" (p. 220). This will take too long and be too onerous. Further, there is no agreement on these goals. We don't need yet another list of 100 or more learning goals. States need to highlight a small number of deeply defined core goals (such as literacy, numeracy, and high school graduation) that are in turn related to lateral goals (such as music and the arts, well-being, more-relevant high school programs).

Then, still part of the first component, Hanushek and Lindseth rush accountability in a premature front-end role instead of placing it in perspective as part and parcel of capacity

building (see my discussion in Chapter 4 of intelligent accountability). The placement of accountability as front and center is
understandable given the concerns of politics and the public (and
the dismal performance of the system over the years), but it will
not get the intended results even with better data and incentives.
Hanushek and Lindseth call for "value-added" assessments
(focusing on the gains of students), which is not a bad idea in its
own right. But when they combine value-addedness with the
pressure of transparency, taking stronger action against failing
schools and districts and transfer options, they are back into the
arena of trying to motivate people with more sophisticated sticks
(I will talk about carrots later).

Second, they advocate empowering local decision making—
again, not a bad idea if it alleviates schools and districts from the
onerous bureaucratic piecemeal requirements, but their version
does little to address the low capacity of most of the almost
15,000 local school boards in the county to bring about district-
wide reform. Local decision makers and schools do not need to be
empowered, they need to be engaged. There is lots of evidence that
decentralization will not yield improvement.

Third, direct rewards and incentives, at best, get at partial
individual capacity but do not touch the much-needed collective
capacity that I will develop in later chapters. The authors advocate
performance-based pay for teachers on the grounds that "any
serious attempt to improve achievement has to start by placing
and keeping better teachers in the classroom" (p. 236). I agree
with their intention, but the way to do that is not through rewarding the so-called best, but rather by improving the "working conditions" of teachers (which includes compensation), another idea
I will develop later (see the discussion of performance pay and
better alternatives in Chapter 5). My position does not rule out
extra resources, pay, and so on for principals and teachers to work
in the most difficult circumstances, changing the pay structure to
give beginning teachers higher salaries, providing different routes
to certification, paying teachers according to demonstrated additional expertise objectively assessed, or changing contracts in
order to address incompetence or rigid seniority clauses. But at
the end of the day, better working conditions that affect *all*
teachers are essential for whole-system, not just part-system,
improvement.

Fourth, information, evaluation, and continuous improvement intended "to improve methods of collecting, linking and analyzing data" is an essential part of any strong system as long as it is put to good use. But good data in the service of ineffective strategies becomes bad practice.

The final component of the model is "rational and equitable funding." Again, necessary and valuable in terms of their proposal, but we have seen through Grubb (2009) that money matters only if it is used in combination with compound, collective strategies of the kind in Exhibit 2.1. In short, Hanushek and Lindseth's (2009) solution will send us down yet another path of wasted resources and lost opportunity.

The final consideration of inadequate approaches concerns the aspirations and strategies set out by President Obama and the secretary of education, Arne Duncan. It is a bit unfair to take up the critique in earnest because (1) it is still an early work in progress, and (2) it is extremely difficult for them to change systems from a distance when education is the authority of states, and they control only 10% of the budget. Nonetheless, it gives us a timely opportunity to consider the next phase of reform in order to provide early feedback so that the strategy can be recast to get whole-system reform.

We have the usual "we are going to be number one again" and "the countries that out-teach us today will out-compete us tomorrow." While accepting the Democratic nomination in August, 2008, Obama said, "I'll invest in early childhood. I'll recruit an army of new teachers and pay them higher salaries, and give them more respect. And in exchange, I'll ask for higher standards and more accountability" (Education Week, 2009)—not a bad approach if you can get the chemistry right—and all systems go is precisely about getting the chemistry right.

Obama and Duncan's first cut at the actual policy is not going to be sufficient. Arne Duncan (2009) has been presenting to various groups—national governors, national teacher unions—what he calls his four-pillar plan. In particular he calls for

1. A robust data system that tracks student achievement and teacher effectiveness;

2. Improving teacher and principal quality through recruitment, training, and rewarding excellence;

3. Turning around the 5,000 worst-performing schools in the country (out of the total 100,000), including taking the ceiling off the number of charter schools, presumably so they could help tackle this problem; and

4. The development of higher standards and assessments in which every state and states together would set internationally benchmarked standards and assessments.

There is also the massive investment of stimulus funds through the American Reinvestment and Recovery Act (ARRA), with big money—$100 billion for K–12 education—within which, for example, there is money for "Race to the Top" innovative proposals ($4.35 billion to states and $635 billion for district innovation). We have already seen that big money by itself is a waste—predictably squandered.

The stimulus money, *in the absence of an appropriate whole-system reform conception,* will fail. Merely filling out the Race to the Top (R2T) application will take each state 642 hours to work through the 35 pages of draft guidelines (McNeil, 2009). There is already evidence that states will find ways to use stimulus money to alleviate budget cuts in other areas, and even if the money is spent on intended strategies, these strategies themselves (the four pillars) are incomplete, partial remedies. On top of all this, the stimulus money is "one time only," not built into base budgets. You can spend a hell of a lot of money in a short time if it is only for buying ad hoc solutions. I repeat, these are early days and revisions are being made as I write these paragraphs—see below for one significant revision to the R2T application guideline requirements.

Let's take the pillars one by one: A robust data system is necessary, especially linked with higher standards and assessments (pillars one and four). If done according to plan, the sheer number of goals and standards would be reduced, they would be stronger (higher-order goals and standards), and they would be uniform across the country (no more set your own standards no matter how low). These two pillars are essential, *but only if they come with capacity-building strategies.* So far, the latter is missing, but again see below.

Pillar two, improving teacher and principal quality, is certainly the required centerpiece of any system reform. Every top-performing system in the world is characterized by high-quality teachers and principals (Barber & Mourshed, 2007). But in these countries, it is the *entire profession* that makes the systems tops. Arne's second pillar is useful, but when you look closely, it is an *individualist and partial strategy.* We need a comprehensive pillar that includes improving working conditions that make all teachers quality performers.

Finally, turning around the 5,000 schools is a worthy goal, but I am going to say that it is not just these 5,000 units that need to be improved but also the contexts in which they work. This is why in our turnaround strategy (Chapter 4) we take the school and its district as the unit of change—all schools, not just the laggards in isolation. If you want system reform, it is not just 5,000 schools that need to improve but also the vast majority of all schools in the system—90,000 or so—not just 5,000. You must change the context in which these schools are operating—the whole system is implicated.

It is noteworthy that between the first draft of this book and the current version that the R2T criteria were revised to include a fifth component. Added is a "State Success Factor," which consists of a coherent state reform agenda, capacity to lead local district reform, and ability to improve student outcomes. (U.S. Department of Education, 2009). This is presented as the first of the five sets of criteria, and it is worth 25 points out of 100 in assessing the proposals. But saying so doesn't make it so. And the application guidelines for the 4.35 billion are 148 pages of single-spaced three-column details with a complicated point and subpoint system. Striving for complexity and achieving clutter, when the goal should be to focus on the action-oriented "skinny," which is the essence of successful and deep reform (see Chapter 3 and Fullan, 2010).

The Center for Education Policy conducted a survey of state leaders' reactions to the ARRA stimulus package (Center for Education Policy, 2009). Predictably, they found that "States appear to be more certain about their plans to fill the first two ARRA assurances [standards and data systems] that are more easily accomplished by state actions than they are about the two [increasing teacher effectiveness and turning around low performing schools] that depend on local politics and conditions" (p. 2). This survey was conducted prior to the addition of the fifth pillar—coherent agenda and capacity to lead local district reform—which requires even more rapport between state and local strategies. The biggest complaint that the state leaders had concerned "the multiple or inconsistent reporting requirements and . . . the lack of state capacity" to put the plan together (p. 3).

Thus, the solutions being attempted by Obama, Duncan, and other large-scale reformers are based on a badly flawed model because they have little chance of mobilizing the collectivity to engage in joint reform. Hansen (2009) nails this problem when he characterizes modern management as "the enemy of [effective] collaboration":

> Managers and management thinkers celebrate decentralization, which works like this: you delegate responsibilities for operations, products . . . and geographies to a group of managers. The clearer the lines of responsibility, the better. You then develop objectives and metrics for each manager so that he or she knows what to achieve each quarter and year. To improve the chances of success, you give the managers considerable freedom—they run their own unit. Then you hold them accountable for their results and put in place incentives to motivate them to reach the objectives. Bonuses, salary increases . . . and promotions go to those who deliver. Those who do not deliver are coached or let go. Predictably, each manager of each unit works hard and focuses on reaching their targets. You sit back and marvel at the beauty of the system. (Hansen, 2009, p. 49)

Hansen makes clear that this system delivers *up to a point* (p. 49). Now the flaw:

> The problem is that each manager becomes increasingly independent and tries to maximize his or her unit—after all, that is how the job is defined. Managers care about reaching their goals and have little interest in helping others achieve theirs. Over time, decentralization risks turning a company into a loose collection of units, which become fiefdoms or silos. (p. 49)

Hansen has captured *the antithesis of collective capacity.* You may get subcollective capacity, such as when a school collaborates internally or collaborates within a cluster of schools, but you will never get whole-system reform. It is deceptive because it works to a point. You get short-term improvements. I think that this is what is happening in the New York City model and in New Orleans. Paul Vallas and Leslie Jacobs (2009), for example, characterize the race-to-the-top lessons from New Orleans as consisting of four key strategies: school-accountability legislation; chartering of new schools with rigorous screening for quality; unequivocal embrace of parental choice; and staffing schools with mission-aligned, talented educators. Does this sound like Hansen's modern management that is the enemy of broader collaboration? Don't get me wrong, it does some good, stops the bleeding, gets examples of individual school improvement, and even overall tests scores go up for a while. But, this approach will never get whole-system reform because it actually does not work on the whole system cultivating the collective capacity that would be required to accomplish the goal of moral purpose for all.

Linda Darling-Hammond (2010) has drawn essentially the same conclusion. Darling-Hammond documents the dreadful decline in teacher quality and its unequal distribution. In California, for example, the proportion of unqualified teachers in schools with the lowest achievement quartile (high minority and poverty) is 25% compared to 5% in the highest quartile (p. 41). In Texas, between 1996 and 2002, the proportion of teachers who were certified when they entered teaching declined from 86% to 47%, and "most of those who entered without training were teaching in high-minority, low-income schools" (p. 93). We will return to Darling-Hammond later, but essentially her solutions are similar to those presented in this book. We must shift, she says, "from enforcing procedures to building capacity [and] from managing compliance to managing improvement" (p. 270).

As I said, these are early days, but all previous big reform efforts since 1983 (all of which have failed) had their early days as well. Obama and Duncan are going to have to figure out how to partner with states and to engage in the development of whole-state-reform efforts, which build the collective capacity of the entire system—a topic I address in Chapter 5. States in turn are going to have to establish whole-system reform strategies that partner with all districts and regions within the state. To do this, there are a small number of interrelated things you have to do well, and you have to do them relentlessly, getting better and better at it as you go. It is not rocket science, but it is *social science*. Thus is the subject of Part II.

PART II
Getting There

CHAPTER THREE

Collective Capacity at the School and District Level

One version of all systems go (but ultimately not comprehensive enough for our purposes) is when a school district and all its schools get in sync and cause greater student learning across the district. In one sense, we have known quite a bit about this at least since 1999, when Elmore and Burney did their now-landmark study of District 2 in New York City.

There have been various confirmations of Elmore and Burney's original findings over the past decade. My composite compilation of the findings is in Exhibit 3.1. Only a small minority of districts evidence these characteristics, but when they do they generate widespread and potentially sustainable capacity to raise the bar and close the gap of student achievement.

As true as these findings are, they apparently do not get to the root of the strategy as evidenced by the fact that they are not catching on (i.e., we are not finding widespread implementation of these features). The depiction of districts on the go must be more fundamental and more dynamic. This is the purpose of this chapter.

I take four examples of whole-district successful reform in three different countries: Tower Hamlets in London, England; Long Beach Unified School District in California; York Region

Exhibit 3.1	Characteristics of an Effective School District

1. **Focus:** a clear direction and relentless focus on student achievement through instructional improvement in the classroom. A school board needs a central and singular focus from which all other pieces can flow. A district must continuously strengthen its core by increasing teachers' skills and knowledge, engaging students in learning, and ensuring the curriculum challenges students.

2. **Data:** access and use of data on student learning as a strategy for classroom and school improvement and to monitor progress. Data also help to shape targets for phased focuses of improvement. Data include the development and use of ongoing means of diagnosing student needs and addressing them through specific instructional responses.

3. **Leadership:** development of teacher, principal, and district leadership to share effective practices from each other and from the larger research base. Research is focused on teaching strategies that make a difference in high- and low-performing schools serving similar types of kids. Responses are then developed to deliver job embedded inservice. Leadership roles are defined so that leaders participate as learners in working with teachers to address instructional needs.

4. **Resources:** allocating resources in accordance with this focus without a reliance on one-time, special funding. Resources should be clearly aligned to support the teaching and learning core of the district's work.

5. **Reduce Distractors:** a concerted effort to reduce the distractors that undermine teachers' and principals' capacity to carry out this central strategy. Excessive bureaucracy, inconsistent messages, multiple non-classroom initiatives, and time-and-energy-consuming conflict all distract from the focus of student achievement. Effective districts do not take on too many initiatives at once and are dropping distractors as well as adding things that help them focus.

6. **Community:** link to parents and the community and related agencies to provide support for students and educators and to intervene early in case of difficulties experienced by students and by schools.

7. **Communication:** a constant and consistent communication that focuses on the core message up and down and across the district. Everyone needs to know the central focus of teaching and learning priorities and how to achieve them. Research findings and effective practices need to be shared. Staying on message is crucial.

8. **Esprit de Corps:** a sense of identity and sense of community among teachers and principals and between schools and the district. People take pride in their work and that of their colleagues and feel a strong sense of affinity with the district as a whole. Allegiances are strong, and collaborative competition leverages the schools to stronger and stronger performance.

District School Board in Toronto; and Ottawa Catholic District in Ontario. As noted in Exhibit 1.1, the language of dynamic systems on the go includes precision, specificity, depth, collaborative competition, collective capacity and collective efficacy, and shared responsibility in the context of accountability. It is not alignment that makes all systems go but rather engagement and the power of allegiances put to a higher purpose. Just recently, we are beginning to see other district-wide examples of success that I will refer to below (Dufour, Dufour, Eaker, & Karhanek, 2010; Leithwood, Harris, & Strauss, 2010; Reeves, 2010).

TOWER HAMLETS

The borough of Tower Hamlets lies in East London on the north bank of the river Thames. Its name derives from earlier centuries when the inhabitants of the area were required to provide the yeomen for the Tower of London that remains in the borough at its western edge. Today, it is one of the poorest areas in all of England having absorbed a massive expansion of Bangladeshi immigrants composing 52% of the population. Its 37,500 students are in 97 schools.

I draw here on Alan Boyle's (2009) account that is part of a larger project headed by Andy Hargreaves and Alma Harris called *Beyond Expectations*. Tower Hamlets, one of the most deprived areas in all of England, outperformed the country in terms of growth on every measure of student achievement. On literacy they went from 35% proficiency (for 11-year-olds) to equal the national average of 80% by 2009 (the national figures for the same period were 58% to 80%, respectively). The same is true for math and science, and ditto for secondary school results. They performed way above expectations. How did they do it?

Boyle names four big reasons: resolute leadership, allegiance, professional power, and sustainability. Resolute leadership combines a culture of high expectations where no excuses are acceptable with a school focus on action, "It moves from intention, through specific actions to achievement by setting conditions targets, refusing to be deflected from the core priorities" (Boyle, 2009, p. 13).

At the beginning "resolute leadership, exists in pockets and then is crystallized and mobilized by resolute leadership at the top" (p. 6). When the new director of education, (CEO) Christine Gilbert, arrived in 1997, relationships between the school heads and the district were strained. One of her most significant achievements during her first two years was to build successful partnerships with the schools.

It is interesting and significant to note that the school heads did have a sense of commitment across schools in 1997 (more about this in a moment) but *not with the district*. Gilbert's breakthrough was to make the partnership seamlessly vertical and horizontal around the learning and achievement agenda. High expectations and corresponding achievement were realized through rigorous target setting, capacity building, monitoring, and continuous action.

Second, district leaders and school leaders recognize value and reinforce strong allegiance to each other in the service of a higher cause. There is a willingness to collaborate for mutual benefit that

> Feeds on trust and respect; it demonstrates a genuine collective responsibility with full commitment and loyalty to the cause, not any individual. Its outcomes are coherence and stability; people are passionate in their work and may even be addicted to it. (Boyle, 2009, p. 18)

This is the stuff that makes all systems go. It is tremendously empowering, and clearly collective in its efficacy. Along with strong collegial support among school principals, there is friendly, but definite, competition to outdo each other. Boyle has come to call this *collaborative competition*—a powerful new concept that describes what we have been seeing in dynamically successful systems. People self-consciously collaborate *and* they compete for the betterment of all. This is one of those amazing social phenomena that—when moral purpose combines with allegiance to others—make great things happen. And, it doesn't require heroic efforts. Ordinary people can do it. The energy pie naturally expands. From a strategy point of view, leaders do have to foster and enable purposeful collaboration, but they don't need to do anything about competition (other than being transparent about results and practice) because it occurs naturally as people try to better themselves and the system as a whole.

The professional power that Boyle (2009) talks about is an extension of purposeful allegiance. It includes, says Boyle, "ability and the mental characteristics of confidence, determination and competition to achieve success" (p. 21). It is just as much competing with oneself in order to be as good as or better than anyone else. Once collaborative competition starts, it takes on a life of its own. If the school up the road is doing better than you, you can't help but want to do even better.

Lastly, these three forces of resolute leadership, allegiance, and professional power create the conditions for sustainability:

> As successful strategies and extraordinary efforts become routine, improved performance gathers momentum. Success breeds success among collaborating schools with a shared allegiance. At some point it reaches a critical level where so many schools are moving this way, and supporting each other, that [it becomes] almost self-sustaining. (Boyle, 2009, p. 26)

Sustainability involves four things. One is to establish a large critical mass of "beyond expectations" work that we have just referred to in Tower Hamlets. This has a persistent momentum of its own. The second is to grow, select, recruit, and develop talent (the subject of Chapter 5) consistent with the culture and constantly replenishing it. Central to this is continuity at the top. Christine Gilbert's successor, Kevan Collins, embraces exactly the themes that make Tower Hamlets successful.

The third element of sustainability concerns two related phenomenon—attention to detail and cultivation of innovation and risk taking. Successful organizations are relentlessly consistent with respect to what works while at the same time looking for the next improvement (Fullan, 2008, 2010). Today's relentless consistency is tomorrow's innovation, and tomorrow's innovation is the next day's relentless consistency. Observes Boyle (2009), "for any system to be sustainable, it needs fresh ideas, new ways of thinking and new ways of working" (p. 30).

The fourth requirement for sustainability is for the district to secure itself in its own context. In terms of the community with a steady stream of immigrants from Bangladesh, Hargreaves and Shirley (2009) describe how Tower Hamlets works tirelessly to create new capacity to strengthen relations and engagement with parents and the community. It has done this through working with faith-based organizations, establishing extended services that keep a school open from 8:00 am to 10:00 pm, recruiting community members as teaching assistants and enabling many of them to proceed to full teacher certification.

Another and the biggest element of context is the education system as a whole—the entire country of England in this case. The things that Tower Hamlets are doing are congruent with government policy and enabled by it (such as literacy support). But, not all is rapport. Recently, Tower Hamlets resisted government pressure to set up a City Academy (an opportunity to receive substantial funds to build a new state-of-the-art secondary school). Secondary heads were unanimous in their opposition to the idea of the City Academy because they saw it as a threat to existing cohesion and collaboration, which are essential for continued improvement—a clear sign that "systemness" for all was more important than ad hoc innovation.

LONG BEACH UNIFIED SCHOOL DISTRICT (LBUSD)

Similar in number of schools (but twice the student population) to Tower Hamlets, Long Beach Unified School District has 91 schools and 92,000 students with 50% Hispanic, 18% Black, 17% White, and 9% Asian, Filipino, and Pacific Islander. Also disadvantaged (66% of the students qualified for free or reduced priced meals) and in considerable disarray at one point (Long Beach felt like a war zone in the 1990s), LBUSD has had a long run of success from 1992 to the present (Austin, Grossman, Schwartz, & Suesse, 2004; 2006).

Carl Cohn became superintendent in 1992. His predecessor had practiced a kind of divide and conquer philosophy of "everybody do your own thing." There was competition but no glue. Definitely not an all-systems-go proposition.

Because the system was fragmented and dispersed, Cohn worked on bringing things together centrally with respect to vision, high expectations, and standards. He made it clear that the purpose of central office was to support schools, but to do so through two-way engagement. Like other successful jurisdictions (the small number that are successful district-wide), Cohn made instruction the main focus, such as a K–3 literacy initiative with capacity building through professional-development sessions, new roles for principals, instructional coaches, complete with feedback on practice. Says one participant, "at the beginning the reform process was hard and sometimes very emotional. We weren't used to constructive criticism, and suddenly outside evaluators were giving us critical feedback" (Austin et al., 2004, p. 8)—more about the matter of feedback to teachers at the end of this chapter.

In LBUSD, building the district's capacity for data-driven decision making was a key component in designing interventions and support systems that achieved results. Between 1999 and 2002, the number of fifth graders reading at grade level increased from 6.7% to 53.5%.

Cohn believed in both top-down and bottom-up strategies (not quite an all-systems-go strategy, but headed in the right direction) and in a partnership between the district and the schools. Cohn was superintendent from 1992–2002. Nearly all grade levels demonstrated progress, many quite dramatic. High school dropout rates decreased by two thirds.

We see a touch of collaborative competition in the words of a veteran high school principal, "the expectation of continuous improvement is the same district-wide. There is a friendly competition among the high schools and we know that all of the jobs are hard. We are all expected to be instructional leaders . . . we help each other out whenever we can" (Austin et al., 2006, p. 7). Another principal recalls the preceding year when test scores of a high performing school fell: "As soon as scores were published that principal got a bunch of phone calls from other principals wanting to know what had happened and what they could do to help" (p. 7).

The elementary schools supervisor comments that "it's critical to establish trust and build the day-to-day relationships" (Austin et al., 2006, p. 8). The high school supervisor notes that when they started with the new expectations you could almost hear high school principals thinking, "Yes, I'm an instructional leader because I'm supposed to be an instructional leader, but I'm not quite sure what that means and how I can demonstrate that" (p. 10). And, "five years later I can tell you that 100% of LBUSD high school principals are instructional leaders, why they are and how they arrived there" (p. 10).

Another principal observes that it is not just the lower performing schools that are expected to focus but also "the higher achieving schools on our east side have to figure out how to maintain high achievement," adding, "nobody has an easy ride" (Austin et al., 2006, p. 6).

LBUSD has the strength of social ties and focus built in. Cohn left in 2002, and his successor has carried on in the same direction. Perhaps not as powerfully aligned vertically and horizontally as Tower Hamlets, LBUSD represents another example of whole-system reform at the district level.

Systemic link to the state is another story. California has more than 1,000 districts! LBUSD is only one (it is one of the nine largest districts). Over the years, California has been the classic example of simple resource (one factor) solutions. In 1996, the governor of California suddenly (it seemed) passed legislation to reduce class size in K–3 classes to 20 students or less. Costing billions of dollars, there is virtually no evidence that it has a positive impact on student learning and served, in our language, to be a massive distractor. California continues to be one of the worst examples of piecemeal reform, not to mention the fact that it is currently desperately in debt (it makes you think of all those dollars down the drain). If you are a district in California, the best you could hope for is "one system goes" (your district) or perhaps a group of districts in a county system—if the leadership works on it. We catch up to the role of the state in the next chapter.

Not all districts are amenable to systemic reform. Carl Cohn took his considerable talent and experience to the high profile San Diego City Schools to replace Alan Bersin and Tony Alvarado (of District 2 fame) who had a conflict-filled seven-year run from 1997 to 2004. Doing many of the right things, Bersin and Alvarado left under a cloud of frustration on the part of all parties. Cohn lasted only 18 months in San Diego, during which time his main role seemingly was to reassure the system that there would be no more Bersin/Alvarado reform. Then Terry Grier came from Guilford County, North Carolina. We worked with Terry for four years in Guilford where he had a major impact on student learning and achievement—another instructionally focused superintendent. Terry Grier became superintendent of San Diego schools on March 24, 2008. On August 20,

2009 just 4 days shy of 15 months in San Diego, the Houston Independent School District board voted 9–0 to hire an apparently frustrated Grier to be their superintendent. Some districts never learn—or so it seems.

YORK REGION DISTRICT SCHOOL BOARD (YRDSB)

York Region is a large, multicultural, urban district that is part of the Greater Toronto Area with 130,000 students, 8,800 teachers and 192 schools. In 1999, the new director, (superintendent) Bill Hogarth, stunned the system when he said that all YRDSB students should be reading at the end of Grade 1. There started a 10-year journey of capacity building and deeper still what we call sustainable realization that Lyn Sharratt—the recently retired superintendent of curriculum and instruction—and I have just written about (Sharratt & Fullan, 2009). Bill put together a leadership team that never strayed off message as they built collective capacity.

Once again, we have a combination of strategies that excite people about moral purpose, focus capacity building, and above all develop a strong sense of partnership between the district and the schools, across schools, and between schools and the community. Without strong two-way partnerships and targeted individual and collective capacity building, moral purpose would only be a slogan.

The core of capacity building was 13 parameters that the school and the district developed together (see Exhibit 3.2).

There is no need to discuss the 13 parameters except to say that school teams and district staff work together (through professional-learning sessions and day-to-day job-embedded work) to implement the parameters in all schools and classrooms. I talked from the outset about the sine qua non importance of *collective* capacity building—the team, the group, the organization, and the system working together to get better. A visitor can go into any one of the 192 schools in YRDSB and have similar conversations—the language of focused instruction is ubiquitous. A principal or vice principal can move to a new school and find a critical mass of kindred spirits. It is noteworthy that we have recently added a 14th "wrap around" parameter called "shared responsibility and

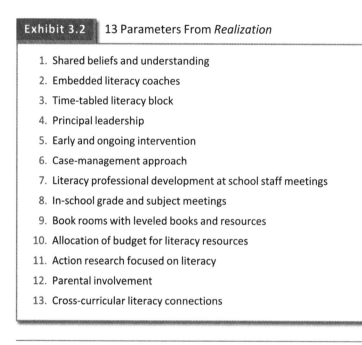

Exhibit 3.2   13 Parameters From *Realization*

1. Shared beliefs and understanding
2. Embedded literacy coaches
3. Time-tabled literacy block
4. Principal leadership
5. Early and ongoing intervention
6. Case-management approach
7. Literacy professional development at school staff meetings
8. In-school grade and subject meetings
9. Book rooms with leveled books and resources
10. Allocation of budget for literacy resources
11. Action research focused on literacy
12. Parental involvement
13. Cross-curricular literacy connections

Source: Sharratt & Fullan, 2009, p. 15.

accountability," which is none other than our intelligent account-ability (see Sharratt & Fullan, 2009). With focused collective capacity building, accountability to a large extent gets internalized in the group and in its individuals.

Karen Louis, Ken Leithwood, and associates (2009) reported findings from their Wallace Foundation study of leadership in a sample of nine states, 43 districts, and 180 schools. One of the most powerful sources of the district influence on schools and students was the development of school leaders' "collective sense of efficacy" about their work. The commentary could have been written precisely about YRDSB when the authors concluded.

Districts contribute most powerfully to principals' collective sense of efficacy by:

- Establishing clear purposes that become widely shared;
- Unambiguously giving priority to the improvement of instruction;
- Providing flexible, varied, meaningful, and just-in-time professional development for both school administrators and their staffs;

- Assisting schools in the collective interpretation and use of data for decision making. (Louis et al., p. 84)

Collective efficacy means that people have confidence in each other. Principals trust, value, and depend on their peers. School leaders and district leaders similarly believe in each other's capacity, individually and jointly, to solve problems and make progress. Allegiances develop but so does collaborative competition. Collective capacity is more than the sum total of individual capacities. It is a qualitatively different phenomenon, and one that most reform strategies fail to appreciate (see Chapter 2). And, it is a powerhouse because it compounds individual efficacy into collective capacity and impact. This is not hypothetical. I am talking about what actually happens in practice.

You see the results evidenced at the individual school level. Crosby Heights is a K–8 school of 662 students in a low-income neighborhood. When Principal Ryan Friedman arrived five years ago, he found no common focus, a negative culture, a facility in poor shape, unsafe school environment, critical parents, and on and on. With high expectations and careful capacity building within the school, and external learning connections to other schools and the district, in three short years the school dramatically improved. On the provincewide tests conducted by the independent Education Quality and Accountability Office (EQAO) (2009), in three years, reading scores went from 44% to 90%, reaching the ambitious provincial standard; writing went from 40% to 87%; and math went from 50% to 83% (as measured by the progress of the same cohort of students from Grade 3 to Grade 6). Ryan and his colleagues did this by focusing on the 13 parameters, respecting the collective agreement, getting union leaders on board as key supporters, and incorporating job-embedded learning "between the bells" as he called it—a seemingly astounding result but this was accomplished by ordinary teachers focusing and being well led.

Jill Marr is the principal of Armadale Public School, the district's largest elementary school, serving a highly diverse and multilingual community with over 80% of the students Tamil, including a continuous flow of immigrants who arrive without any English. Jill started by cleaning up the building—all six custodians were replaced—and organizing resources. This was done in the first six months. She then used the parameters to construct and integrate a plan of action. The specificity and precision (two of our new watchwords of success) of what the school is doing is amazing. Here is a partial list:

- Job-embedded professional learning, based on student needs, has increased the consistency of practice within and among classrooms. Teachers are modeling lessons in one another's classrooms on a monthly basis.
- Professional learning is active in each division. The identified focus is assessment-based instruction with teacher moderation of student work.
- Teachers are using a variety of assessment tools and instructional strategies to meet the learning styles, interests, and needs of every student.
- Teachers are building class and student profiles and attending case-management sessions to identify high-yield strategies.
- Teachers and students can clearly articulate what the learning targets are and what success criteria are needed in order to achieve the targets as evidenced by daily-literacy walks.
- Two groups (of five teachers each) are engaged in action research and meet bimonthly to review their data and actions.
- The majority of staff, 98%, have volunteered to participate in a biweekly professional book club and bring supporting student evidence to the discussions.
- An increase in the usage and frequency of centralized resources has been observed.
- Student needs are at the forefront when making budget decisions.
- Attendance at family and community schools events has increased by 200%. (Sharratt & Fullan, 2009, p. 87–88)

As far as the bottom line is concerned, the school has zeroed in on the students at risk (those at level two or below on a four-point scale). Staff at given grade levels know these students by name and by targeted learning action. Amazingly, in *one year*, the number of students at risk has been reduced from 378 to 233, and this has occurred in each of the nine grade levels, K–8. More impressive are the achievement results in literacy and numeracy.

In one year (2008 compared to 2009), Grade-3 reading went from 63% proficiency to 84%, writing went from 75% to 91%, and math went from 76% to 89%; there was the same pattern for Grade 6, 58% to 77% for reading, 66% to 78% in writing, and 60% to 72% in mathematics. This is a remarkable sweeping of the table, given that it represents only one year of work in a disadvantaged school with almost 1,000 kids. When I asked the leadership team of 10 how the speed of change felt, one member said, "Like a freight train that we were almost in control of." Another said they were able to move so rapidly because they focused on a small number of things and knew what to do specifically. The collective effort carried the day. This phenomenal result was accomplished because of focused leadership in the context of a highly supportive and engaged district-wide culture. It represents "the speed of quality change" as leaders grasp the skinny of change effectiveness (Fullan, 2010).

These two schools are not unique. York deliberately builds whole-system, all-schools reform. They work continually on what I would call the *social glue* of capacity building—the collegiality and instructional practices that enable them to pull together. Good practice produces commitment. Committed people pursue even better practices. The scaffolding to do all this operates at three permeable levels—the district, the subnetworks of schools, and the school/community.

At the district level, the literacy collaborative contains the overall framework of shared vision and related capacity building, involving the 13 parameters. Professional-learning sessions with leadership teams from all schools take place several times a year (schools are in one of four cohorts because of the large numbers). The same message and two-way communication about purpose and progress occurs throughout. An annual literacy fair—in which all 192 schools in the district prepare and share 25-minute multimedia accounts of what they set out to do for the year and what they accomplished—reinforces the substance of what they are doing and strengthens the collective identity and commitment to the overall endeavor.

The next level is more operational. Every school belongs to a geographically organized learning network (LN) consisting of from six to ten schools in a cluster. There are 22 LNs. These school networks focus on specific practices, student results, cross-school sharing, learning to do better, and mutual commitment. They engage in collaborative competition with each other and with the rest of the system. When they meet, participants consist of school principals and leadership teams, the superintendent (who is the coordinator of the LN), and district curriculum consultants. If you observe an LN session, you will see that no one dominates. They are colearners, with practice and results as the drivers. It is noteworthy that the director (Superintendent) of York Region, Bill Hogarth, delayed the setting up of the LNs for seven months despite strong pleas from his area superintendents because he wanted to make sure that whole-district commitment was in place, thereby trying to avoid LNs becoming isolated fiefdoms. Effective leaders always have an eye on allegiance to the system as a whole while they also support smaller-scale, intensive learning partnerships. Most recently, purposeful high school networks focusing on particular themes have been established, again strengthening both capacity building and peer and district allegiances.

The third element is the school where the principal and other school leaders become even more operational in professional learning communities working on similar agendas in ways particular to the needs of their students and communities.

The overall effect is that ideas, leadership, and commitment flow readily across the three levels. York has a high trust, transparent learning culture where mistakes are treated as part of growth, and moral purpose (all kids can learn) is taken seriously by all.

It works. York Region District School Board, despite being one of the largest, most diverse districts in Ontario, is one of the best. It has raised achievement scores across the six provincial measures of reading, writing, and math for Grades 3 and 6 by some 15% over the past five years, along with increasing its Grade-10 literacy scores and its high school graduation rates. And when progress seemed to plateau a couple of years ago, York stayed and deepened the course. In 2009, when the scores again jumped up, the excitement around the district was palpable. It seems that the struggle itself makes gains all the more satisfying.

Currently, York is addressing the difficult question of sustainability and establishing the conditions for continued development in the future. Two ideas crystallized from this consideration. The first is what we now call "the 14th parameter"—*the shared responsibility and accountability* that is built into the interdependent practice within the system. We will return to the role of accountability; but for now, let me say that a powerful feature of all systems go is that shared commitment, allegiance, and responsibility for results becomes collectively owned. This is "realization" giving it a life beyond particular individuals.

The second element for sustainability concerns the systematic recruitment, selection, and development of new teachers and administrators. This topic is the subject of Chapter 5, but I'll say here that the key points are that this individual capacity development must be focused and systematic, and above all it must be integrated with (part and parcel of) the daily collective work of the schools and the district. Qualifications frameworks of leadership qualities reinforce the daily job-embedded work; they don't cause it.

Finally, unlike the previous two cases, YRDSB is nested within an all-systems-go environment that includes the other 71 districts in the province and the government. York readily contributes to and learns from other districts as part of the provincial strategy to improve the whole system. To show that York Region is not unique in Ontario, we will also examine Ottawa Catholic District School Board in the next section. In both cases, York and Ottawa, they are successful largely in their own right; but more significantly for systems reform, they are successful because they are integrally connected to a provincewide whole-system reform strategy—a critical matter that I take up in the next chapter.

OTTAWA CATHOLIC
DISTRICT SCHOOL BOARD

Jamie McCracken, the director (CEO) of Ottawa Catholic District since 2003, was a high school principal in the district and worked in the district office prior to his promotion. He describes the culture back then with one word, "clenched." The director issued 13 thrusts annually that were supposed to be the themes for the year. Each year, there were a different 13. Jamie learned that he never had to "thrust back," as there was no follow through. He ran a good school, but he knew that it was totally detached from the district and his colleagues. He was hired to change that.

Jamie and his coleaders have used virtually every major theme that I have covered in this book—the ideas in Exhibit 1.1, the day-to-day work of Irina Fedra and Albert Quah that I described in Chapter 1, the strategies in Exhibit 2.1, and the nature of the work seen in York Region. And they did it without any direct outside help other than drawing on good ideas and taking advantage of new resources.

The Ottawa Catholic District School Board is one of 29 Catholic districts (of the total of 72) in Ontario's public education system (Catholic districts are fully publicly funded as per the Canadian constitution established at the time of federation). The district has approximately 42,000 students in 78 elementary and 15 secondary schools. The demographics in the catchment area, being in Canada's capital city, range from affluent to disadvantaged including large numbers of immigrants who arrive without speaking any English.

Jamie started with some large-scale meetings that he called "reimagining days." For the first time in the history of the system, he included nonprofessionals—support staff, custodians, technicians, and bus drivers. Knowing something about our emphasis on a small number of goals and staying the course, he selected three core priorities: success for students (e.g., ensuring high levels of critical literacy), success for staff (e.g., building Catholic collaborative learning communities through shared leadership), and stewardship of resources (e.g., aligning human and operational resources to support and close gaps in student achievement). These have been the same three priorities every year for the past seven years. They replaced the 13 or so annual random thrusts of the previous regime.

The system glue—the same kind we saw in York—is fostered in three interrelated ways: constant communication with all groups, precision-based capacity building and problem-solving strategies, and a careful pursuit of personnel policies and recruitment of leaders who are selected and developed to serve the three core goals. Jamie has built in two-way communication sessions with all groups—principals, teachers, support staff, parents and community, and union leaders. He sees all 4,000 employees as his constituency. He knows about one of our "skinny rules"—communication during implementation is far more important than communication prior to implementation (Fullan, 2010). Keep the message simple, keep it focused and consistent, and keep conveying it, and talk about the results, the problems, and the strategies as you go.

With respect to the second means of focusing—precision-based intervention—there are a host of interrelated strategies that are under way. The central district structure and personnel were revamped to get rid of previous silos so that leadership could operate as a guiding coalition—again, with the same message and emphasis on the three basic goals of the district. He introduced a critical-literacy framework similar to York's 13 parameters, requiring schools to focus on literacy by building their individual and collective capacity. This was not invitational; it was presented as nonnegotiable. The system provided all kinds of support in terms of resources, coaches, data access, smart goals, time for job-embedded learning, and the like. There was an atmosphere of risk taking and learning, as long as you were focused on solving problems with respect to the core priorities.

The system got increasingly specific. The buddy system I described in Chapter 1 (where teachers and students in Grades 1–3 are buddied with their counterparts in Grades 4–6 for a buddy day once a month) is used by most schools in which teachers coplan and coteach to improve literacy and math.

The system has become more and more focused. For example, they discovered that the 10 largest elementary schools were, for the most part, doing "good" but not "great." They were getting respectable results in the low 70s at level three and four. As Jamie put it, "I suspected that not much had changed in their approach. I challenged these principals to look at their instructional practice and challenge teachers to move to the more-focused approach involving personalization, precision, and professional learning" (Fullan, forthcoming). Jamie shared the C. D. Howe report with them that compared school results in the province by comparing like districts with like districts. The C. D. Howe analysis had concluded that these particular schools should be getting much higher results because of their demographics. The schools with help from the district responded to this challenge. Several of these schools have much better results in 2009 due to this pinpointed focused intervention that is typical of highly effective districts.

Similarly, in September, 2007, the district started the "engagement project," which targets students showing signs of decreased school engagement. Based on indicators of student tracking and achievement results, six schools in the district were selected to participate. Four youth workers were appointed to the position of engagement coach. The role of the engagement coaches is to personally connect with the students regularly, assist with behavioral interventions, help with learning strategies, make home visits where necessary, participate in team meetings to review cases, and liaise and collaborate with community agencies. The results from the evaluation of the project show a decline in absences, lateness, and suspensions. Key intervention strategies that worked included providing students with alternative learning experiences, individualizing programs for students, as well as monitoring and maintaining regular contact with students.

Another powerful intervention is the Senior Kindergarten Tutoring Program (Ottawa Catholic School Board, 2009). The program involves identifying five-year-olds who are seriously behind in oral language and literacy skills. The program runs from September to June and consists of an extra half day of learning five days a week over and above the regular kindergarten program. Four qualified teachers, appointed to the position of tutor, implemented a variety of programming activities and learning experiences that were all viewed through the lens of oral language. The results from the program, using a quasiexperimental design, showed that the program was successful for all students, both male and female, and was especially beneficial for English-language learners. By spring, the students in the tutoring program outperformed or performed similarly to the comparison group on most of the assessments. Further, these students were already beginning to show transfer of emergent literacy skills to reading with some students attaining the district reading targets for Grade 1 before the end of the first term.

All this work on instruction is buttressed with basic, always focused, professional learning communities within schools and the use of networks of schools—such as the math network, in which several schools are learning from each other—linking better instruction to better results.

Thus, there are a host of activities under the label that I have called "precision-based strategies." There is one more major reinforcer of cohesion, and that concerns personnel policies and leadership recruitment and development. Jamie is blunt with vice principals, telling them that if they want to get promoted in this system they have to be curriculum and instruction leaders. He started to identify future leaders by "tapping them on the shoulder" and getting them into future leaders programs. The district always has a list of 15 to 20 names of teacher-leaders, vice principals, and principals who would make strong instructional leaders. There are also leadership programs for support staff and maintenance staff. The whole system, including custodians, knows what the three key goals are and how the system is doing relative to results. And how are they doing?

From 2005 to 2009, all six scores (Grades 3 and 6, reading, writing, and math) have improved from around a baseline of 60% for the six scores to 66% (Grade-3 reading), 75% (Grade-3 writing), 76% (Grade-3 math), 74% (Grade-6 reading), 74% (Grade-6 writing), and 69% (Grade-6 math). They have the greatest gains in the province when you look at all 45 districts with more than 500 students taking the test. Grade-10 literacy results are 89%—well above the provincial average. When the 2009 results came out in August, 2009, showing from 2% to 9% increases over 2008, Jamie put the results up on a slide at a meeting with all school principals. As the cheers arose, the superintendents entered the room carrying trays of glasses of champagne to celebrate the accomplishments. This district is not finished and remarkably is well on its way to eliminating the achievement gap between socioeconomic classes.

The leadership at Ottawa Catholic at both the district and school levels is preoccupied with improving student achievement. It is almost all they talk about—strategies, what results are we getting, and what specifically more can we do. It is about the whole child. Jamie McCracken, as director, inherited the running of a "social justice fund." Its three priorities were facilities, technology, and poverty. Guess what? Prior to Jamie's management, it never got around to poverty (too amorphous or daunting?), and its $60,000 base more or less stayed as is. Jamie changed that. He eliminated the first two priorities and invited all employees in the system to donate to the social justice fund. It works this way: Any principal can put in a request for a small-scale poverty related item—food, clothes, epi-pen, and so on, and Jamie commits to responding with the money within 24 hours. That fund is now steady at $350,000 per year and is spent down every year.

All of this development and success at Ottawa Catholic is occurring because they have mastered the small number of key things that make all systems go. They combine a relentless focus (always on message), precision high-yield instructional strategies, focus on data and results, and the cultivation of leadership at all levels to engage everyone in the moral purpose of improvement for all. The leadership in Ottawa Catholic is self-conscious about achieving alignment and focus in their daily work, an alignment that they are able to convey on one page consisting of the Director's messaging to all leaders and employees: reinforcement by superintendents of the priorities at regular families of schools meetings; interdepartmental cooperation at the district level; district reorganization, where program and staff development have been combined into one student success department; continuous leadership development focusing on instructional leadership; school-improvement planning and school reviews; and planning for learning in which new big ideas in evidence-based strategies are sought and cultivated. In short, this is how you make the whole system go.

We are also seeing a small number of other districts mastering the art and science of accomplishing whole-system reform. Two sets of such districts just documented in the United States are described in Dufour and colleagues (2010) and Reeves (2010). Dufour and colleagues name the schools and districts, clearly specify what they are doing, and provide extensive evidence in each case about the substantial impact on student engagement and achievement. Adlai Stevenson High School, Illinois; Boones Elementary, Virginia; Prairie Star Middle School, Kansas; Lakeridge Junior High School, Utah; Highland Elementary School, Maryland; Cinco Ranch High School, Texas; Kildeer Elementary School District 96, Illinois; Whittier Union High School District, California; and Sanger Unified School District, California—all schools and districts that depict the precision and specificity of comprehensive, coherent focus that get results.

These schools and systems display a relentless attention to clarity of purpose, collaborative cultures, collective inquiry, action orientation, commitment to continuous improvement, a focus on results, strong leaders who empower others, willingness to face adversity, conflict, and anxiety, and perseverance in the face of obstacles (Dufour et al., 2010). These leaders have all had to overcome initial obstacles through persistence, resilience, and flexibility (see also Fullan, 2010).

All are precise and systematic in the way we have just seen, working collaboratively on (1) exactly what is it we want all students to learn, (2) how will we know when each student has acquired the essential knowledge and skills, and (3) what happens in our school when a student does not learn (Dufour et al., 2010, p. 6). All are impressively and measurably successful, from Adlai Stevenson that has improved results every year in virtually every indicator for a quarter of a century (p. 65), through Kildeer Elementary School District in Illinois with its seven schools ("we wanted absolute clarity of language . . . principals need a deep . . . understanding of key terms," states Superintendent Tom Many [p. 131]) whose performance has steadily climbed from 86% to 96% proficiency on all state tests, to Sanger Unified School District whose 19 schools have gone from 20% proficiency on state tests in 2001–2002 to 59% in math and language arts (p. 160).

Doug Reeves (2010) arrives at a similar conclusion and warns us about coming up short. His four-level implementation audit scale furnishes revealing results. He shows that with respect to each level one to three (within which more and more staff are implementing a given program—but not 90% or more) that there is *no* linear impact on student achievement. It is only at level four, when there is 90% or more participation in deep implementation, that there is a payoff in student achievement. He found that low implementation is worse than no implementation and that in any case it is only when there is virtually full implementation that the impact is substantial—another confirmation that "all system reform" is the only thing that counts. Reeves also confirms that focus is key, and that we need to worry about our "not to do list" as we zero in on a coherent, consistent reform implementing a small number of core priorities especially well. When schools and districts do this he found that triple 90% and even triple 100% is achievable (schools that have 90% *plus* poverty, 90% *plus* minority, and 90% *plus* achievement on state proficiency tests). A warning here however—proficiency on state tests is not a deep measure of achievement, so we must be cautious about declaring any victory.

In any case, all of this is encouraging; but two further problems remain: only a minority of districts are successful; and a more serious problem is that hardly any states (whole systems) are even close to becoming this good.

SOME SYSTEMS GO

There are four points in concluding this chapter: (1) very, very few districts have the focus and coherence of Tower Hamlets, Long Beach, York Region, Ottawa, and those reported by Dufour and colleagues (2010) and Reeves (2010); (2) accountability works in whole-system reform by increasing collective capacity and shared responsibility and reinforcing it through the use of transparent data and positive intervention; (3) let's not forget the micropicture where students, parents, teachers, and administrators are, and (4) the solution is "not a program"; it is a set of strong focused practices and norms.

Grubb (2009) conducted an exploratory study of 12 schools in California concerning their use of resources relative to impact on student learning. In terms of district-wide focus, Grubb states, "no district in our sample had developed a coherent approach . . . applicable to all its schools" (p. 184). Later, he cites Elk Grove, Oak Grove, Rowland, and Long Beach as districts that do have their act together:

> high performing districts that have developed a balance between centralized policies and decentralized or school control—a district version of distributed leadership, with a role for schools to play in district decision making . . . They also developed processes for shared learning among schools. (p. 234)

Remember, however, we are only talking about 4 districts out of over 1,000 in California. There are other individual, district-wide examples of success in the United States—as we have just seen. And, Childress's (2009) brief account of Montgomery County, Maryland, is another case in point. Despite these individual successes, I would venture to say that less than 5% of districts in the United States operate with the collective capacity that we have seen in the previous section. In Canada, that percentage would be double or more but still be distinctly in the minority. In short, most schools in the United States are in districts that waste resources, aided and abetted, however unintentionally, by state and federal departments.

My point, to be taken up shortly in Chapter 4, is that district coherence and focus is critical, but it will only occur on a large scale if the state is working on this agenda with the same relentless focus that we see in the best districts. Whole-system success will be accomplished not when states run district reform directly but rather when they will act analogously to how the best districts interact with their schools—namely, through partnership and leveraging good work that is already going on in pockets with school leaders and teachers who are ready to share, and then making sharing and development more widespread as others find the experience exciting and motivating.

Second, where does accountability fit in? For the districts and schools in this chapter, the strong arm of accountability is attached to your own body and those of your peers. This internal school and district accountability is ubiquitous in these organizations—a requirement that Richard Elmore (2004) calls "internal accountability." You don't start with blatant external accountability—you end with it. Because it is internally driven, these schools quite comfortably work with the external-accountability frameworks. I will talk in the next chapter about intelligent accountability and what to do with schools and districts that are not making their way to internal accountability, but the gist of the answer is that no effective accountability holds unless it is practiced and reinforced as a collective responsibility.

From a policy perspective, Andreas Schleicher (2009b), the head of OECD's PISA unit, tells us that the highest performing countries:

> Strike a different balance between using accountability tools to maintain public confidence on the one hand, and to support remediation in the classroom aimed at higher levels of student learning and achievement on the other. These cornerstones have gone beyond systems of external accountability towards building capacity and confidence for professional accountability in ways that emphasize the importance of formative assessment and the pivotal role of school self-evaluation. (p. 3)

Exactly!

Third, let's not forget the microworld of the everyday teacher and principal. Grubb (2009) documents what he calls "dynamic inequality":

> What really counts for many dimensions of adult life is dynamic inequality—the inequality among students that

develops over the long years of elementary, secondary, and then post-secondary education. Students start school with initial differences, many of them related to class or family background, and these differences widen steadily (at least in this country [the U.S.]). By the twelfth grade, the differences among individuals are enormous: some students have dropped out and are still reading at the elementary school level while others . . . are about to enter the best universities in the world. (p. 10–11)

Teachers working in failing schools can't possibly be having a good time. It is no fun working in a negative culture, especially when the moral stakes are so high. The best ones leave, others give up and slip into the deadening miasma (along with their students) of hopelessness. The evidence shows that teachers will respond to authentic opportunities to develop individual and collective capacity and the strong moral power of allegiance to their peers related to a higher cause. In fairly short order, those that shouldn't be there will leave, others remaining will start to thrive, and they will be joined by newcomers attracted to inspirational possibilities.

All it will take to reverse this tragedy is the discarding of distractors and waste while introducing the handful of powerful factors I am identifying in this book. It is not easy, but it also is not a mystery. In addition to their quantitative analysis in providing country-by-country benchmarks of performance in literacy, math, and science, PISA has begun to dig deeper into the cultures of more- and less-successful schools and countries. They have found, for example, that "teachers value feedback they receive from school principals and colleagues as fair and helpful, with real impact on their classroom practices" (Schleicher, 2009b, p. 2). Schleicher also found, as did Hattie (2009), that teachers feel that they do not get enough valuable feedback during their work. He goes on to say,

There seems much greater scope for teachers to learn from other teachers with teachers reporting relatively infrequent collaboration of the teaching force within the school . . . Improving this will require adequate pedagogical leadership as well as effective human resource development policies in schools. (2009b, p. 3)

Fourth—and this is crucial—Dufour and colleagues (2010), Elmore (2004), Reeves (2010), and I are all crystal clear on one matter: *The solution is not a program; it is a small set of common principles and practices relentlessly pursued.* Focused practitioners, not programs, drive success. Neither off-the-shelf programs or research per se provides the answer. Professionals working together with focus is what counts. The beauty of this is that it is the group that owns the solution, and that is why it is more sustainable. What I am finding in our work is that the strongest solutions consist of going from practice to theory. Effective practitioners are critical consumers of research and not implementers of research findings.

On the bigger scene, there is the classic chicken-and-egg dilemma. Neither side, policymakers nor professionals, trust each other to get it right. Right now, we have a stalemate in most jurisdictions. Somebody's going to have to take some risks (see Chapter 6). If I were a betting man and this was the stock market, I would invest in the state or province that focuses on the small number of complex factors that make all systems go—the win-win pie will expand exponentially and pay dividends for generations to come. This is exactly the time when states and countries must get their policies and strategies for educational reform right. We know increasingly a great deal about the dos and don'ts of such system reform—the focus of Chapter 4.

CHAPTER FOUR

The State We Are In

There are only five things that leaders need to remember and do, albeit concretely and with relentless integrated intensity (see Exhibit 4.1), and one thing to avoid—stop doing the wrong things: They are wasteful distractors. Limit the number of core initiatives.

Exhibit 4.1   Making All Systems Go

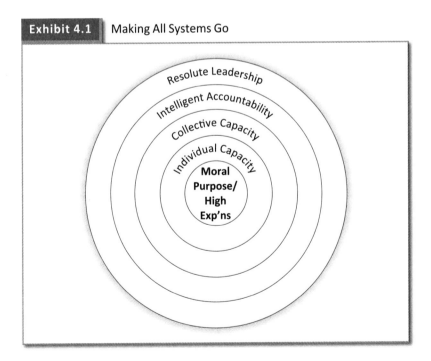

In our economic language, these five components represent a complex resource, one that compounds and multiplies its effect through interrelated use. Five is not much to remember. Indeed, all-systems-go savvy takes the mystery out of complexity.

I apply this thinking first and foremost to a whole state or province. It speaks to whole-system reform, all three levels of school and community, district and region, and state. In the final section of this chapter, I address the federal role, but success or failure stands or falls on the capacity of the state or province.

MORAL PURPOSE AND HIGH EXPECTATIONS

Every state espouses moral purpose—on paper. The particular brand for all systems go has several components that I will lay out here. To be realized, moral purpose must, above all, be self-consciously and explicitly played out through the other four components in Exhibit 4.1.

Moral purpose focuses on raising the bar and closing the gap for all children and youth in society relative to those dispositions and skills essential for surviving and thriving in a complex, interdependent global society. Second, moral purpose goes on to specify the key standards—core ones relating to literacy, numeracy, and the evolution of 21st-century skills that I referred to in Chapter 1. In this respect, Arne Duncan's (2009) fourth pillar, "the development of higher standards internationally benchmarked" is on the right track provided that the list of standards does not get too long. Third, the moral purpose that I am talking about is dead serious about *high expectations for all*. People with this sense of moral purpose really do believe that every child can learn given the right approach and amount of time. And when they see this confirmed day after day in the most difficult circumstances, they believe it even more deeply. And, they have history on their side. For example, we now have more students graduating from postsecondary institutions than people 50 years ago believed were capable of finishing high school. And kids with disabilities that were kept out of schools 30 or 40 years ago are now reaching quite high levels of achievement. High expectations for all, thus, are realistic (if only you believe and do something about it).

It is revealing to note how moral purpose is activated. Some teachers and principals have it intensely from the beginning of their careers. Most teachers come into the profession because they want to make a difference in the lives of students. They want to contribute to the future life chances of individuals and to the prosperity of society. But I would say that in some extremely difficult situations, some teachers and principals, deep down, may not believe that "these particular students" can or will learn. What will convince them? It turns out that it is not moral exhortations or mounds of evidence from other similar situations that have been successful. Rather, it is when these teachers and principals are helped to get success with their own specific students. Teachers become believers (and their moral commitment and energy zooms) when they themselves experience and are part and parcel of significant new achievements (Fullan, 2010; Sharratt & Fullan, 2009). More about this in the next chapter when I focus on teacher incentives that work—but actually accomplishing something is the best incentive around for doing more of it.

Moral purpose consists of the triumvirate of raise the bar, close the gap, and clear, uplifting standards and high expectations for all. It is a no-excuse commitment to deliver on the promise of developing a higher-performing and more-equal society. Moral purpose is society's god, except in this case the glory of god is you, your peers, and citizens around you. We have seen (Chapter 1) through Richard Wilkinson's and Kate Pickett's (2009) analysis that more equal societies come out better on virtually every measure that counts.

In all systems go, moral purpose and high standards are not something stated up front as a general wish. Moral purpose is powerful when it is embedded in all strategies and actions. Every policy, strategy, and action through the other four components in Exhibit 4.1 should be designed and experienced in a way that automatically and relentlessly reminds people every day that education reform is a matter of moral purpose of utmost importance to us individually and collectively; and as I have said, this gives people the experience that it can be accomplished through deliberate all-systems-go strategies.

You know that you are on the right track when many different things you do by way of strategy all trigger moral obligation and responsibility to do better. I am not talking theory here. The question is not whether strategy is intended to generate morally grounded action (all policies seem to intend this) but whether it *actually does*. It is only what works that counts. Leaders who are committed to making the whole system go must carry forward moral purpose deeply into the remaining four components of our framework.

RESOLUTE LEADERSHIP

Dalton McGuinty, premier of Ontario, is in his seventh year in office. From minus day one he was not only committed to making whole system improvements but equally was concerned about how to get there. We will see some of the results of this effort later in this chapter, but let's visit him now that he has had the experience of trying to accomplish this in the entire public system—two million students, 4,900 schools, 72 districts, and a society of 13 million people.

On June 30, 2009, McGuinty delivered a speech to the Global Education Competitiveness Summit in Washington, D.C. He cited seven lessons that come from his immersion in whole-system reform (see Exhibit 4.2).

This is resolute leadership. It is about purpose and action. Under Lesson One, McGuinty says that "teachers and principals can smell a fad a thousand miles away," and thus the proposed focus "has to be an enduring, government priority backed by resources and an intelligent plan." In Lesson Two, he observes that "if I, as premier, did not take a personal and active interest in driving academic achievement, progress would come to a halt."

Exhibit 4.2

Lesson One: The drive to make progress in our schools can't be a fad.

Lesson Two: Education reform is not important to your government unless it's important to the head of your government—personally.

Lesson Three: You won't get results unless teachers are onside.

Lesson Four: Don't forget the hard part: You must improve your teaching.

Lesson Five: If you want to achieve your goals, you need to keep up the pressure all the time.

Lesson Six: Once you start making progress, you've got permission to invest more.

Lesson Seven: The best way to sustain your effort to improve schools is to keep it personal.

Source: McGuinty, 2009.

He doesn't mean that he goes it alone. Resolute leadership means building the "guiding coalition," the core group who meet frequently around purpose, progress, and corrective action and are always on the same page even when there is disagreement. In this case, the core team is the premier, the minister, the deputy minister (highest ranking bureaucrat, equivalent of the state commissioner), their policy staff, and me, as special advisor. Thus, resolute leadership becomes an organization or system phenomenon— literally the organization pursues reform and its results relentlessly.

In Lesson Three, McGuinty notes that it doesn't matter how much money you spend or how much you want change, you have to figure out how to build a positive working relationship with teachers. This is not easy. Given the history that most teachers and their unions have had with past reforms, they are naturally guarded about the current ones. In effect, resolute state leaders say that we have to figure out how to trigger and reinforce the moral purpose and responsibility of teachers because we can't get whole-system reform without it.

The fourth lesson taps into another vein of wisdom for the *effective* resolute leader because it concerns the improvement of instruction. This has very much to do with individual and collective capacity that we will get to shortly. McGuinty puts it this way:

> Sure, you can have world-class standards, rigorous testing and brilliant data management so we know precisely how each student is faring—but you still have to improve your teaching. (p. 6)

Lesson Five was keep up the pressure—all the time. By this, he meant that you must keep your eye on the ball, stay the course in this respect, and constantly be alert to deflecting distractors. Address distractors quickly and effectively so that the only real issue left is instruction and learning. Limit the number of priorities.

Lesson Six captures the positive momentum of investing on top of success. It is necessary to kick start the reform with new money (for capacity building, for instance). If you have the right strategy (basically, Exhibit 4.1), you will get some success (within one year in our experience). It doesn't take much success to legitimize additional budget. The public welcomes investment provided that it is measurably paying off. In whole-system reform, success can be modest at times as long as it is steadily progressing. In Ontario's case, improvement on most measures is only about 2% per year, but it does add up.

INTELLIGENT ACCOUNTABILITY

Intelligent accountability (of course no one is in favor of unintelligent accountability) was a phrase first used by David Miliband in 2001 when he was secretary of state for education in England. I am not sure exactly what he meant by it, nor probably was he, but now that we have had some good experience with whole-system accountability, we can be more precise about it.

Accountability is needed in order to reassure the public that the system is in good hands and progressing well; it is also needed to help implementers know how well they are doing while providing the feedback and help to do even better. Our concern here is with what actually works to move the whole system along—not what should work, but what does work. Intelligent accountability in essence involves building cumulative capacity and responsibility that is both internally held and externally reinforced (see Exhibit 4.3).

The first five on the list make the sixth component less needed—or to put it differently, reserved for special cases.

Recall McGuinty's Lesson Three—you won't get results unless teachers are onside. So, the practical question for all systems go is what approach to accountability is going to get the vast majority of teachers onside—*onside* being defined as doing the things that get results.

Exhibit 4.3	Intelligent Accountability

1. It relies on incentives more than on punishment.

2. It invests in capacity building so that people are able to meet the goals.

3. It invests in collective (peer) responsibility—what is called "internal accountability."

4. It intervenes initially in a nonjudgmental manner.

5. It embraces transparent data about practice and results.

6. It intervenes more decisively along the way when required.

Let's start with a simple example. Thomas Homer-Dixon (2009), complexity theorist, wrote an article in the *Toronto Globe & Mail*, in which he addressed the question of how to get people to behave at work with greater environmental sensitivity. Drawing on a small experiment from one of his colleagues, Homer-Dixon made the following observations.

First, he states (as intelligent accountability does) that people generally respond more readily to carrots than to sticks, that they tend to avoid risks (especially if judgmentalism is in the air), and that they act faster and more readily when they have easy access to information about how their behavior compares to others.

In the experiment, Homer-Dixon's colleague went around (in a nonjudgmental, nonthreatening manner) and asked people to have their office practices monitored, rated, and publicly advertised. A color-coded badge was then posted outside each office indicating that person's progress in reducing his or her environmental-impact behaviors.

As Homer-Dixon reports, a friendly competition developed to see who could do the best. Doing well became a matter of pride and reputation, and new norms started to take root. Most importantly, participants' use of resources like paper and energy and their output of waste dropped sharply.

Sticks, of course, can get us to change behavior, but as Homer-Dixon says, "we won't change with any enthusiasm" (p. A15), which means that the changes are less extensive and creative than they could be.

You see in this modest example that the accountability gets built into the culture. It is powerful. This is what I mean by *internal* or *intelligent accountability*. Although Homer-Dixon doesn't comment on this, imagine that one or two office workers don't take up the new habits. My guess is that peer pressure is going to be far more formidable than if the boss issues an order or comes on with the office environmental police.

If you want accountability to serve an improvement role, you have to realize that positive incentives are far more powerful than negative ones. On a bigger scale, we have built this accountability philosophy into the regime in Ontario. People know the moral purpose and the corresponding high expectations, and they also know that there is going to be resolute pursuit of the consequences of strategies employed.

Once expectations are identified, we invest in the power of capacity building (improving instruction), peer interaction, identifying and spreading best practices, and transparency everywhere. In this very process, internal accountability does a great deal of its work. People generally get more motivated when they are helped to become more effective and see positive results. They feel the excitement and the pressure of collaborative competition, which brings both allegiance and attempts for them to outdo each other for a common moral cause.

Two other aspects of intelligent accountability bring to bear overall system seriousness to the endeavor. These involve how to handle turnaround schools and turnaround districts. Given that the system is driven by high expectations and resolute leadership, it is no surprise that it follows through on individual, local, and system performance. If a system is to improve overall, it needs a turnaround school and turnaround district strategy as part of its repertoire. What does the intelligent accountability version look like?

As part and parcel of an all-systems-go mindset (Exhibit 4.1, in total), the government, through its literacy and numeracy secretariat in the Ministry of Education established its intelligent accountability strategy called Ontario Focused Intervention Partnership (OFIP)—note the emphasis on *partnership* (with schools and districts).

Schools are identified as low performing or static based on the results from the province's testing agency (the Educational Quality and Accountability Office—EQAO). By policy, EQAO assesses reading, writing, and math for all Grade-3 and Grade-6 students, resulting in six measures annually per student (but just for these two grades). Those schools showing low or stagnant scores over three years (this is key, not one year, but a three-year window) are seen to require different types of assistance than schools that are improving. This is nonjudgmental—capacity building first, judgment (if needed) later. There are three groups of OFIP schools:

- OFIP 1: Where fewer than 34% of the students are achieving at least 3 or 4 (Level 3 is the provincial standard) in literacy and numeracy in two of the past three years; it is worth noting that because of the success of overall strategy there are hardly any OFIP 1 schools remaining.
- OFIP 2: Where 34% to 50% of the students are achieving the provincial standard, with results being static or declining.

- OFIP 3: Where 51% to 74% of the schools are achieving the provincial standard, with results being static or declining based on three-year trends.

Right away, you notice something different. This is not Arne Duncan's bottom 5,000 schools (5% of the total) or a given state's list of worst schools. It includes OFIP 3 schools, which are essentially cruising schools that are doing okay but going nowhere. Overall, there are 1,000 schools in OFIP—25% not 5% of the total. The significance of this is twofold. First, if you want whole-system reform, the message must go out to all schools, not just the so-called failing ones. Second, and more subtle, if you try to change the bottom 5% you won't change the *context* in which they are working. All systems go basically says that all schools are implicated. The spotlight is on everyone, and this is what makes it work as a system endeavor.

As to the particulars, OFIP improvement strategies focus on the implementation of high-impact classroom strategies (see Chapters 1 and 3) that support individual student learning. Since OFIP began in 2006–2007, the literacy and numeracy secretariat has invested $25 million each year in OFIP, plus an additional $8 million for OFIP tutoring initiatives (before- and after-school tutoring for students).

The intervention plan includes the district as well as OFIP schools. The work between the Ministry, the schools, and their districts is indeed a partnership in which, together, leaders analyze student-achievement data, provide intensive assistance in instructional practices, and assess, monitor, and evaluate the impact of improvement strategies.

The results show the impact of intelligent accountability practices (carrots over sticks, capacity over cajoling). Evidence shows that OFIP 1 and 2 schools improved at a significantly greater rate than other schools. For example, from 2006 to 2008, the overall rate of increase for the province as a whole is about 2% per year (itself quite a good whole-system accomplishment across the 4,000 schools), while OFIP schools typically increased by around 10% on average (the actual range over the six scores is 3%–16%, with most scores showing double-digit gains). And as noted, there are hardly any OFIP 1 schools remaining. The OFIP strategy, unlike many turnaround school strategies in other jurisdictions, includes districts as partners, which means that district capacity building is part of the strategy—that is, building up the internal accountability (responsibility and capability) of the district as part of the outcomes. This potentially has more lasting effects.

So far, you have not heard me talk about any legal authority. We have relied largely on the support and pressure of direct capacity building and transparency. In this way, the internal system (all schools and district) feels the presence of carrots and normative sticks. This notwithstanding, legal authority and intervention needs to be part of intelligent accountability (the main point is you don't lead with intervention, you follow with it). The province recently passed new legislation (called the Provincial Interest Regulation) that enables it to intervene in districts where there is persistently low or stagnant academic performance, although only after various other steps toward improvement have been taken. This will now be on the books as a regular part of the accountability system. It is good to have this big stick as a later, if not last, resort. When it is used, it will be used in a way similar to OFIP, namely, to build the internal capacity and accountability of the district.

Intervention would include temporarily taking over the school board and district. You know that intelligent accountability is operative when, if such a takeover occurs in a given situation, it is accompanied by an attitude from peers (other districts) and the public that is akin to "it is about time that the Province took action." Intelligent accountability has widespread legitimacy.

Linda Darling-Hammond (2010) has drawn essentially the same conclusion. Some states, she observes, "believe [that] the major problem is a lack of effort and focus on the part of educators and students, and that standards and tests will motivate change if they are used to target punishments to those who fail to meet them" (p. 73). Whereas what is needed, she argues, is for states and districts to act on "the theory that improvements depend on greater teacher, school, and system learning about more effective practice, combined with more equal and better targeted resource allocation" (p. 73).

It is not, then, whether to have standards and assessments that is the question, but rather the crucial variable is *how they are used.* You get more authentic and powerful accountability paradoxically by getting at it indirectly through collective capacity building in which teachers are helped, individually and collectively, to focus on instruction. The question is what is going to motivate *all teachers* to become engaged in the solution.

COLLECTIVE CAPACITY BUILDING

I said on the first page of the preface that collective capacity is the breakthrough concept to make all systems go. When you look closely, most governmental policies mistakenly focus on individualistic strategies (how to reward excellent teaching, how to develop and support new principals, etc.). These are necessary but not nearly sufficient conditions for reform, and I will put them in perspective in Chapter 5. Collective capacity is much more powerful and is the sine qua non of system reform.

Almost all of us who ended up receiving a strong education can recall one or more teachers who cared just a little extra, who reached us at a critical time and literally altered the direction of our lives. These teachers are to be prized for changing our lives for the better. But, there are not enough of them. They don't add up, as seen from the stagnant results of the U.S. school system over the past 30 years. Collective capacity is essential because it produces many more quality teachers who operate in concert.

Better education, strange as it sounds, is not produced by individual teachers working with one student or one classroom at a time. It is coproduced by teachers and students across the years. Learning is a joint effort of lots of people working together on a given day and cumulatively over time.

Grubb (2009) makes the case convincingly when he observes that instruction becomes engaging only under certain conditions:

> When it is based on forms of learning whose relevance is clear; when it uses a wide array of students' skills and interests; when it poses appropriate challenges to students; when it allows for some student choice and autonomy; when schools develop close relationships between students and adults; when instruction allows students to take an active role in constructing meaning; and when programs are well structured with clear purpose. (p. 185)

It is clear that these are *collective* resources. They are improvements that teachers cannot make working alone. Recall the Grubb argument that we must go beyond simple resources (one factor at a time) to compound (two factors) or complex (three or more) resources. In other words, effective resources are most often collective. Compound resources, "by definition require decisions about two or more resources simultaneously and are therefore likely to require cooperation from several decision-making sources" (p. 227).

The power of collective capacity is that it enables ordinary people to accomplish extraordinary things—for two reasons. One is that knowledge about effective practice becomes more widely available and accessible on a daily basis. The second reason is more powerful still—working together generates commitment. Moral purpose, when it stares you in the face through students and your peers working together to make lives and society better, is palpable, indeed virtually irresistible. The collective motivational well seems bottomless. The speed of effective change increases exponentially. Collective capacity, quite simply, gets more and deeper things done in shorter periods of time.

Remember, we are not talking about one school at a time. This is about system change, all schools. It turns out there are a cluster of concepts involved—collective capacity, collective efficacy, collective competition, and colearning. In Chapter 3, we examined York Region District School Board in Ontario and its "system" of 192 schools. We saw how they foster district identity through the learning collaborative that met and reinforced moral purpose, good practice, and whole-system mindsets for the district as a whole. They also break this down into local learning networks—22 of them—in which clusters of six to ten schools work together on the details. These learning networks consist of school leaders (principals and teacher leaders) and supervisory officers (line authority superintendents and staff support—curriculum consultants from the districts). They focus on instruction and on the development of all schools in the network. They simultaneously have a local and district presence. And here is the clincher: When you see them meeting and addressing problems, and you observe the participation of the various leaders, *no one person is in charge.* They operate naturally as colearners with great focus but no hierarchical leadership.

And they compete—within the learning network (who is making the most progress), and across the district, evidenced by the dynamic learning fair held each June when teams from all 192 schools demonstrate what they have accomplished during the year.

We also saw how the Ottawa Catholic District, using increasingly strong and pinpointed intervention strategies and related capacity building, is on the road to virtually eliminating the achievement gap associated with socioeconomic status. And, they did this coming from nowhere.

But this is the district level, and we are talking in this chapter about the state—all 72 districts, and the Ministry of Education government in the province. At the state level, there are two big issues, one concerns whether the government gets its own act together internally; the related other matter pertains to how it goes about relating to the field.

We are talking here about capacity building and the first-order question is whether the State Department or Ministry of Education has its own capacity house in order. It may seem obvious, but it takes capacity to lead capacity. Most state departments, including Ontario's Ministry of Education in 2003, do not have the capacity to lead all systems go, which is the enterprise of helping the whole system focus on instruction, assessment, correction, and instruction on a continuous basis in all schools and in all districts. In a word, states normally do not have the *domain knowledge* required for this work. Second, they tend to operate as bureaucracies, which means there is too much paperwork, too many rules, arcane communication, and the dreaded silos (think uncoordinated octopus).

The first thing to do then—and this is crucial but very hard to do—is to change the culture of the state department, adding new capacities. We have done this in several ways since 2003. First, we established the guiding coalition of premier, minister, deputy minister, and their policy assistants who meet regularly to establish and maintain focus. Second, we appointed a new deputy minister (highest ranking civil servant) who had the skill and the charge to change the capacity and culture of the Ministry of Education and its units. (To rest my case that such a person was up to the task, read Ben Levin's [2008] account of how to change 5,000 schools; Ben was the deputy minister who led this transformation). Third, we needed to add domain knowledge, so we created a new unit, the Literacy and Numeracy Secretariat (LNS) within the Ministry of Education—some 100 people, many of whom were highly respected instructional leaders in the field.

Throughout this book, we have seen the modus operandi of LNS (and later we added a student success—SS—unit to help with high school reform). These are strategies exactly like those in York Region, Ottawa, and their schools, only on a much bigger scale. LNS and SS have partnered with all the districts in the province to do the all-systems-go capacity building and intelligent accountability work that results in student improvement. LNS, in partnership with the field, has developed a number of purposeful, specific, network-based strategies to foster deeper and wider implementation. We have already referred to the schools on the move strategy that identifies schools that are making significant progress, and makes it easy for others to learn from them. There are several networks, such as one where several districts are working together to identify best strategies to address the educational needs of aboriginal students. Then there is the leading school achievement (LSA) project that partners LNS, the three principals' organizations (public, Catholic, and French), and Curriculum Services Canada to work on strengthening leadership focus on instruction and results through greater "trilevel" alignment—school, district, and province, working with 1,200 schools across 46 districts (Leithwood & Jantzi, 2008). All of these efforts are focused on the same agenda—literacy, numeracy, high school reform, and graduation, and all serve to reinforce and synergize the collective capacity necessary to get whole-system reform.

For an interesting twist, examine Exhibit 4.4, which displays the overall and trend results on our six key measures per elementary school—Grade-3 reading, writing, and math, and Grade-6 reading, writing, and math. But, here we show 12 scores because we are comparing the 60 English-speaking boards with the 12 French-speaking boards, all of which are fully publicly funded.

Exhibit 4.4   EQAO Provincial Results, 2008–2009

English	EQAO 2008–2009	Change From 2007–2008	Change From 2002–2003
Grade 3			
Reading	61%	0	+11
Writing	68%	+2	+13
Math	70%	+2	+13
Grade 6			
Reading	69%	+3	+13
Writing	67%	0	+13
Math	63%	+2	+10

French	EQAO 2008–2009	Change From 2007–2008	Change From 2002–2003
Grade 3			
Reading	66%	+6	+19
Writing	76%	+2	+18
Math	66%	+4	+19
Grade 6			
Reading	77%	+2	+19
Writing	79%	−1	+16
Math	80%	+2	+14

You will see that the system in total has moved forward steadily since we introduced the all-systems-go strategy—some 13 percentage points across 4,000 schools (following five years of stagnation, 1998–2002, prior to our strategy). But notice the French. They have outperformed the English districts by some five percentage points (18 percent gain over most measures, instead of 13).

It is difficult to draw causal connections between strategies and practices on the one hand, and impact on the other, but here is what we think is happening (which, in effect, corroborates my contention that collective capacity is hyperpowerful). The 12 French districts are a close professional community. They see a joint purpose in protecting the viability and success of French-language education by demonstrating quality. This broader purpose is one shared by leaders, teachers, parents, and the community. These districts support and pressure each other with purpose and intensity around lifting results. Also, full-day junior and senior kindergarten (four- and five-year-olds) has been a reality for a number of years. Combined with a clear focus on oral language development, young students are better prepared for success in literacy and in school.

There are many ways in which the 12 Francophone boards problem solve, develop, and share together and with the province. To name just a few:

- The French-language Education Policy and Programs Branch's (FLEPPB) *tourneé provinciale* team allows each district to have a face-to-face meeting with Ministry representatives and have an open discussion about red flags in district performance. The 12 French-language districts exchange resources and practices with respect to information management, data analysis, and practices that improve student achievement.
- Provincial and regional capacity-building sessions coordinated by LNS have resulted in the sharing of strategies and resources. District and school leaders are invited to share their best practices. Networking is an important component both during and in between sessions.
- Three districts representing three regions have been working on a common approach to better principals' instructional leadership. The material and the research from this project have been made available to all French boards.
- The three French districts in the eastern region have jointly developed an eight-volume math resource document entitled *Les Apprentissages Essentiels en mathematiqués,* which aligns instruction, learning requirements, and assessment for all grades. All 12 districts use these important resources.

Well, you get the picture. These districts are sharing and trying to outdo each other and the other 60 districts in the province all for a common cause. In short, this is collaborative competition whereby schools focus around a common, collective purpose and help each other (while competing with each other) to race to the top.

A similar but less-pronounced difference occurs within the 29 Catholic districts compared to the 31 other public districts (all publicly funded). They too have a distinctive mission and collaborate and compete with each other and with the system as a whole.

My point is this: Moral purpose and a sense of urgency has generated the need and opportunity for a more creative and, perhaps counterintuitively, a more collaborative approach to programming and sharing effective practices. And the province, "the system," has developed a strategy to enable and reinforce collaborative competition. I said before that you don't have to stress the competition component. Moral purpose plus capacity building, plus transparency of practice and results, plus an emphasis on collaboration all serve to generate natural and healthy competition.

So, the French have the common cause of minority status. The Catholics have religion. And the public system has, well, its own secular god, namely *society*. Society's god, so to speak, is the moral purpose of doing well as a society, the commitment that one has to peers (a moral commitment) and the personal moral commitment that teachers have in making a difference to students. Individual and societal well-being and prosperity have great moral draw provided that the conditions to enact them are evident.

The system as a whole—all 72 districts—does well because of common moral purpose and collaborative competition to leverage each other upward through knowledge of effective practices and the pressure of outdoing each other for a critically important common cause. It comes a little more readily to the French and the Catholics because they have a more available common cause, but the lesson here is that the public system also has a common cause and can do even better than they are by mobilizing the power of collective moral purpose and the learning and commitment that comes from developing collective capacity and efficacy. The extra-ordinary energy to make all systems go is in the collectivity, not the individual members working alone.

INDIVIDUAL CAPACITY

I take up the role of individual capacity in detail in Chapter 5, so we need only to make the main points here—one negative and two positive. First, my criticism is that policymakers overestimate and overuse individualistic strategies. It is understandable but ineffective. To think that you can change the culture of the teaching profession by attracting individuals of better quality misses the fact that only collective action will be strong enough to change systems. So, the warning is do not over rely on individualistic strategies.

Second, individual capacity building is still an important part of the solutions, and there are effective and ineffective ways of going about it, which I sort out in the next chapter.

Third, and most pertinent to this chapter, it is essential that individual, organization, and system strategies be closely aligned and integrated. Far from expecting individualistic strategies to carry the freight (my criticism above), we must make individual and collective strategies work in synergy. For example, if you want instructionally oriented principals, you need to focus on developing collective cultures that make this the daily work, thereby producing more such school leaders as you go (i.e., the topic of Chapter 3 and this chapter), *and* at the same time personnel policies and professional development must be precisely aligned to reinforce and extend these qualities in the pipeline of new leaders coming down the pike.

To be specific, standards and qualifications frameworks for leaders must capture the new role, promotion criteria and decisions must be based on the new requirements, and mentoring and induction programs for prospective and new school leaders must be developmentally sound. But these elements are not a substitute for, but a supplement to, the direct work required to change the collective cultures. The sequence here is crucial. Do the real work of change in the day-to-day culture of the system, and *reinforce* it with individualistic strategies; don't expect it to work the other way around. In short, individual and collective strategies are compound resources, and only the two together will make the system go.

THE ROLE OF THE FEDERAL GOVERNMENT

Arne Duncan has an enormously difficult job. He is expected to help lead the United States from its current position of around the 21st in the world in education attainment to becoming number one again. He is expected to raise the bar and close the gap. He is, in a word, being asked to make the United States a more equal society. Yet, he controls only 10% of the budget and faces a constitution that grants states the authority over education policy, not to mention the 15,000 districts, many doing their own thing.

The implication of our analysis for Duncan is that he must figure out how to further the state agenda discussed in this chapter. This is a matter of helping to "frame and deliver"—both have to be done in partnership with states.

Duncan is already moving down the framing path. In the United States, this requires establishing a single set of consistent, high quality, small in number, core standards—this is, in fact, one of his four pillars (see Chapter 2). Improving the student information system, another of the pillars, is essential, provided that it is geared for use as a strategy for improvement.

But, it is delivery that is Duncan's weak suit, not just because it is daunting—which it surely is—but because there is no strategy for collective capacity building, which is the essence of effective delivery. Since he can't do this directly, it must be done through the state. In much the same way as Ontario relates to its districts, the feds must relate to the states. As I noted in Chapter 2, the revision of the regulations for the Race to the Top 4.35 billion dollar competition has recently added a fifth component: the coherence and capacity of the state to work with local districts to bring about system reform in the state.

This is welcome news. But, the theory of action to really do coherent and shared capacity building is particular, and I have tried to set out the particulars in this book in the clearest, most-specific terms. This represents a massive cultural change in the way that governments—and the United States in this case—go about leading system transformation. This is the essential task and challenge facing federal and state governments. And a further word of warning, the stimulus funds of billions of dollars do not themselves provide the answer. Everything in my change theory (coming from practice, incidentally) tells me that great fanfare prior to doing something is fragile. Genuine, deep excitement can only be realized by doing quality change on the ground. That is the central task, with stimulus money only being a blip along the way.

Thus, ongoing partnerships with (initially) selected states willing to go all the way are necessary. The outline of this endeavor would require that the federal department of education organize itself and its culture so that it can work politically and technically with states. Given the senior leadership appointments made by Duncan within his department, there are signs that this is happening, although there is no indication yet that his office has forged its own "guiding coalition" and corresponding theory of action based on the agenda proposed in this book.

Delivery, then, requires ongoing partnerships with states where federal and state counterparts work these ideas through, initially and especially, *during implementation*—problem solving and refining as they go. This will not come naturally politically or otherwise for many states, but what the federal government needs is a few good examples across diverse states on which they can build. A sharp awareness and involvement with international benchmarks such as OECD's PISA, which the United States has largely ignored until recently, will be helpful.

The resolute leadership that we discussed in this chapter will be essential from both the Obama administration and the state governors. Moral purpose must become a natural driver, not the empty rhetoric of No Child Left Behind, but rather moral purpose that causally links capacity to outcomes. Moral purpose is both a cause and an effect. The more it is realized, the stronger it gets as a powerful impetus for ongoing reform.

There are many good things going on in pockets of the United States; the challenge now is to invest in federal-state partnerships that are designed to build collective capacity for whole-system reform. Because the U.S. has been performing so poorly, focusing on a small number of proven interrelated strategies (see Exhibit 4.2) could bring early wins, which in turn could be leveraged for more progress. It is always easier to follow a bad act. Awakening and giving moral purpose an effective outlet through increased capacity that gets better results would galvanize groups to get and build on breakthrough achievements. Leaders can change the state we are in, but only if they jettison bad habits and specialize in a few good, new ones.

The new federal-state partnership in Australia that focuses on literacy and numeracy across the country might have some useful lessons along the way, although it is beyond my scope to consider it here, and too early to tell how it will fare. If the National Partnership in Australia is to be successful, federal and state leaders in that country would be well served to heed the advice in *All Systems Go*.

My main message, in short, is that either at the level of each state, or at the federal-state interface, leaders must grasp and pursue the essence of collective as well as individual capacity building. The theory of action embedded in Exhibit 4.1 is the essence of this work. The rewards will be exponential, much more powerful than any strategy that moves only parts of the system.

CHAPTER FIVE

Individual Capacity Building

The top performing countries in the world draw from the highest 30% of the university graduating class to stock the teaching profession. They also assess, as a ticket of admission, "suitability to teach" (strong moral purpose, commitment to continuous learning, and desire to work collaboratively in teams). The United States, at best, draws from the middle 30%—probably even lower.

In this chapter, I am going first to criticize individualistic strategies and then praise them in perspective; ending with a discussion of incentives that work—ones that are compatible with the claims in this book, namely, incentives that are based on collective capacity building while incorporating individual teacher development on a large scale. To anticipate my conclusion, it is going to take the United States 20 years to transform the teaching profession *provided* that they combine individualistic and collective strategies. This is not a complaint about individual teachers: It is a system problem that will require a system response.

It is true, as a South Korean Minister of Education observed, "the quality of an education system cannot exceed the quality of its teachers" (Barber & Mourshed, 2007, p. 16), but therein lies the beginning of the individualistic fallacy that focuses on individuals as the answer (not to mention that some of these policy solutions are downright wrong).

THE CRITIQUE

On performance pay, who are you going to believe in the following accounts, Hanushek and Lindseth (2009) or Pfeffer and Sutton (2006)?

Recall from the previous chapter that Hanushek and Lindseth (2009) recommended a five-part solution, one part of which was "direct rewards and incentives" including merit pay. Here are a couple of their assumptive principles:

- The system should reward those who contribute to success—for instance, those who bring about high achievement.
- Rewards should be based on each person's contribution to success to the maximum amount feasible. (p. 218)

And,

There is growing *research* to show that rewarding successful teachers is one of the most important steps a school district can take to improve achievement. A bipartisan group called the Teaching Commission, headed by Lewis Gersten, the former chairman of IBM, found that "our current compensation system fails our teachers and our children." (p. 237–238, emphasis added).

Then,

There it is, pure and simple: pay teachers based on their performance, *as do virtually all other professionals*, or forget about improving student performance (p. 238, emphasis added).

Compare the above with Pfeffer and Sutton (2006): "Before telling you the results of all that research [on merit pay] we can illustrate how you can figure out if merit pay will or won't work" (p. 22). They then suggest we ask ourselves the following questions:

- What assumptions does the idea or practice make about people and organizations? What will have to be true about people and organizations for the idea or practice to be effective?

- Which of these assumptions seem reasonable and correct to you and your colleagues? Which seem wrong or suspect?
- Could this idea still succeed if the assumptions turned out to be wrong?
- How might you and your colleagues quickly and inexpensively gather some data to test the reasonableness of the underlying assumptions?
- What other ideas or management practices can you think of that would address the same problem or issue *and* be more consistent with what you believe to be true about people and organizations. (p. 22, emphasis in original)

Pfeffer and Sutton list a couple of the assumptions about teacher "pay for performance" plans:

- Teachers are motivated largely, or at least significantly, by financial incentives; so pay for performance will induce greater and more effective effort.
- Teaching is a solo activity—there is little interdependence with others in the school. (p. 23)

They then save us time by cutting to the chase:

It turns out that merit pay for teachers is an idea that is almost 100 years old and has been subject to much *research* . . . that *evidence* shows that merit pay plans seldom last longer than five years and that merit pay consistently fails to improve student performance. (p. 22–23, emphases added)

Who is more convincing? Hint: Pfeffer and Sutton's (2006) book is called *Hard Facts, Dangerous Half-Truths and Total Nonsense*.

Instead of being pure and simple, let's be compound and complex. There is *no* research evidence to back up Hanushek and Lindseth's claim. Nor do we use pay for performance in virtually any other professions. Almost nobody in human services—doctors, nurses, social workers, police, security guards, bank staff, and so on—is paid for performance (they are paid for credentials and particular expertise, and sometimes for the quantity of service provided). I repeat, no research exists that demonstrates that *widespread* benefits derive from merit pay. A more recent study by business professor Pedro Martins (2009) of financial merit incentives for individual teachers in Portugal (that compared teachers receiving merit pay with several matched control groups over a seven-year period) found that "our results consistently indicate that the increased emphasis on individual teacher performance caused a significant decline in student achievement particularly in national exams" (p. 1). When common sense tells you it won't work, when no research exists that backs up the claim for merit pay (save for small segmented examples where subgroups benefit while the system as a whole suffers), it is time to give up the ghost of merit pay. Collective excellence, as every top performing country has found, is accomplished when you improve the entire profession. As Darling-Hammond (2010) puts it, merit pay for individual teachers "creates temporary rewards that do little for long-term salaries or retention and has been found to be de-motivating to most teachers" (p. 318).

The fallacy begins with the strong and unequivocally true research finding that the quality of one's teacher has a dramatic determining effect on how much an individual student learns. So, the findings go that having an effective teacher versus a less-effective one for three years in a row can alter one's achievement as much as 50 percentile points. And, we also know that teachers are of significant uneven quality within and across schools. The problematic leap in logic comes in deciding how to improve quality. Bluntly stated, you can't do this through performance pay to individuals or even to groups. Donald Campbell (1979) exposed this logical fallacy over 30 years ago when he observed "The more any quantitative social indicator is used for social decision-making, the more subject it will be to corruption pressures and the more apt it will be to distort and corrupt the social processes it is intended to monitor" (p. 85). No amount of direct figuring solves this problem. If you doubt this, try reading Springer's (2009) collection of articles on performance incentives. The evidence of the impact of various types of incentives remains thin, as the solution discussion gets more obfuscated. The problem is the right one—how to get and reward quality teaching—but the solution has to be one where the entire profession is upgraded, as I will discuss below.

None of what I am saying is a defense of the status quo. As I said, we are still stuck with the fact that the quality of teachers is the single most important factor in student learning and that it is uneven at best. As Grubb (2009) put it, "if practices are specific to individual teachers rather than school wide, then students lurch between ineffective and effective practices and experience inconsistent teachers" (p. 207). My point is that you cannot get consistent quality teachers through merit pay (incidentally, Grubb's book is the most comprehensive treatment of money and resources around, and I could not find one word on merit pay in any of its 400 pages).

The message to policymakers is that pay for performance per se will not and cannot get you what you want unless what you want is, at best, tiny pockets of success at the expense of the system as a whole, or, at worse, a win-lose gaming of a performance-based scheme (Campbell's law of corruption). Examine the assumptions and the evidence closely, and you can't come to any other conclusion.

We will get to the solution, but there is one other subtle version of the individualistic fallacy that, although it does produce better individuals, will still not be sufficient. If we take the goals of producing quality teachers and quality principals, which all top-performing systems hold, as Barber and Mourshed (2007) found, a number of recent initiatives are based on sound designs and experience. These programs, whether for teachers or principals, typically focus on instruction, blend theory and practice, provide intensive coaching and mentoring in internships whereby aspirants spend significant time learning about practice in practice, and create cohorts of professionals who learn to collaborate and learn from each other (Darling-Hammond, Meyerson, LaPointe, & Orr, 2010).

In a word, these programs are *job embedded.* Thus, they look like they are collective, but on closer examination they are still individualistic. The assumption is that if we prepare high-quality candidates who will enter the profession or take on leadership positions we will thereby improve the system. These programs are great— that is why I call them necessary—but an ad hoc collection of individuals does not make the whole system go (see Fullan, 2009).

Of course, these new programs are worthwhile. I don't have to cite the evidence that the majority of teacher- and leadership-preparation programs are weak in preparing people for effective service in the profession. Darling-Hammond and colleagues' analysis of eight exemplary leadership-development programs is conclusive that the designs are sound, the experience valuable, and the graduates are better prepared than are those from regular programs.

But when these people—teachers or principals—go into a bad system, they can only make small gains at best. In Darling-Hammond's study, it did not appear that the organizational culture was much different in the schools where exemplary leaders served. To take another example, New York's Leadership Academy is producing high-quality individual principals who are sent to work in hard-to-serve schools. They do some good, which I interpret to be that they "stop the bleeding" (Corcoran, Schwartz, & Weinstein, 2009). In some individual situations, they may even turn around the school dramatically—but this is only piecemeal. It will never add up unless we can also change the culture of schools and schools systems so that the conditions for development are also built into the work itself.

We can also say that high-quality standards and qualifications frameworks (what effective teachers and principals should know and be able to do) are necessary but not sufficient. The good news is that these standards are getting better and more widespread. But no matter how you cut it, they don't develop capacity on the job throughout one's career. Once again, the sequence is wrong—we need instead to focus on doing the work first, and then use leadership frameworks to reinforce and further this work. Thus, individualist strategies, no matter how good, will never result in system change. Let us then do the obvious, *combine* individual and collective strategies with the driver being the latter.

INDIVIDUALISTIC
STRATEGIES IN PERSPECTIVE

There are a whole set of things that are useful for individual development. I have just referred to the value of high-quality preparation programs. Schemes that establish tiers of career advancement based on expertise and on leadership roles outside the classroom also have some merit (see Johnson and Papay's, 2009, report and, in reference to it, Viadero, 2009). Selective use of targeted financial incentives can also work, such as paying teachers more for demonstrated instructional practices they can evidence (for example, the National Board for Professional Teaching standards certification), additional pay for going to hard-to-serve schools, improving salaries including front-end loading of higher start pay, and paying incentive bonuses for subject-area teachers in short supply (such as science or math). Even using incentives to get individuals to go to hard-to-serve places won't by themselves work to get people to stay (how are you going to keep them down on the farm once they have seen the farm?).

But, all of these individualistic incentives are only fed into the fundamental solution which is to change the culture and working conditions in the school so that all teachers are implicated. Thus, if you want to have a "compound" return on your investment (which is the only way to get systemwide reform), you have to combine individual and collective strategies. For starters, let's take a straightforward revealing illustration: Susan Moore Johnson (2004) has spent her career studying how "to find and keep" quality teachers. In this research, she and her colleagues found that a new teacher having a mentor (an individualistic strategy) by itself bore no relationship to job satisfaction and retention, "whereas working in a school with an integrated professional culture is strongly related to job satisfaction" (p. 12). The obvious point is that the culture of the school, itself a collective capacity by definition, is more important, in fact essential, for full success. Ken Leithwood's (2007) research on working conditions of teachers reaches a similar conclusion—to a large extent, the conditions that teachers care about are strongly related to improvement, such as having effective leaders, good colleagues, resources, and opportunities to learn and to build collective efficacy that has a positive impact on students.

Thus, individual capacity thrives if it is integrated with strategies and experiences that foster collective capacity. There is no other way. The top-performing countries have quality teachers, but they have them in numbers—that is, the entire profession or virtually all teachers not just a percentage of selectively rewarded ones.

This takes us back to collective capacity; or one could say, under what conditions would high quality people come to the profession and develop individually and collectively? We have seen these conditions in Chapters 1, 3, and 4, so I will just reiterate them here in different words.

The direct answer to the problem of quality is that it is essential to change the working conditions of teachers and principals. My colleague, Ben Levin (2008), a system leader if there ever was one, shares how he has done this in relation to leadership development. He calls them "seven practicalities."

1. Establishing a vision and goals

2. Building a strong team

3. Creating and supporting the right culture

4. Communication, vision, direction, and accomplishment

5. Recruiting, developing, and retaining leaders

6. Building internal and external support

7. Maintaining the focus on teaching and learning (p. 177)

This is collective capacity building. Let us return for a moment to the basic problem—the development of the teaching profession as a whole. Yarrow (2009) reports on a recent survey on how teachers see the profession. The survey found three categories of teachers: *disheartened* (40%)—teachers who give their principals poor ratings in supporting them as teachers and express concern about working conditions, student behavior, and testing; *idealists* (23%)—teachers who say they became teachers in order to help disadvantaged students, say that good teachers can lead all students to learn, and believe that they have had a positive impact on their students; and, *contented* (37%)—teachers who report excellent working conditions, work in middle- or higher-income schools, and believe they have been efficacious in helping students learn.

What kind of incentive is going to motivate the largest group—the disheartened—while buttressing the other two groups? Not individualistic pay performance. The incentives that work in teaching—as in any helping profession, in my assessment—are related to the working conditions that enable groups to accomplish impressive results that have high moral value. Exhibit 5.1 contains this list.

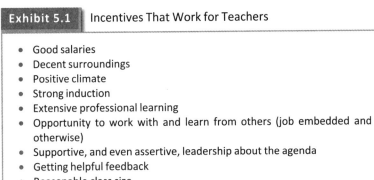

Exhibit 5.1　Incentives That Work for Teachers

- Good salaries
- Decent surroundings
- Positive climate
- Strong induction
- Extensive professional learning
- Opportunity to work with and learn from others (job embedded and otherwise)
- Supportive, and even assertive, leadership about the agenda
- Getting helpful feedback
- Reasonable class size
- Long-term collective agreements (4 years)
- Realizable moral purpose

These incentives leverage all teachers, and they make it increasingly uncomfortable for those who do not improve. Realizable moral purpose is especially effective in reenergizing disheartened teachers. We have found that it is not moral exhortation or evidence that motivates such teachers but rather helping them achieve dramatic success with students that they did not think could learn. The actual experience of success is the turn on that was missing. We can still take action against terribly incompetent and abusive teachers, but it is the middle 40% that must be reached if we are going to get system change. To act this way is a bit more complicated than legislating merit pay, but not all that complex. And the rewards will be powerful and have a self-generating momentum of their own.

POLICY AND STRATEGY

To return to policy and the top-performing system in the world, recall that Barber and Mourshed (2007) found that policies and strategies must focus on three critical components: (1) getting the right people to become teachers, (2) developing effective instructors (including leaders who can do this), and (3) ensuring every student performs well.

For the teaching profession, my central conclusion is captured in Exhibit 5.2:

Exhibit 5.2	The Quality of the Teaching Profession

- Moral purpose (high expectations for all)
- Individual entry (each and every teacher)
- Individual capacity development (each and every teacher)
- Collective capacity development (each and every school, district, and government)

The quality teaching profession takes moral purpose from slogan to sleuthing. It believes that every child, given the right conditions, will learn and that 95% or more of students can become proficient at higher-order 21st-century skills. The profession as a whole believes this, not just because they value it, but because it is committed to and knows that it can deliver on it. Teachers individually and as a group experience success, and it compels them even more.

Policymakers in turn need to know that their job is to make the quality teaching profession a reality. To know that a child's teacher makes all the difference in the world is to know that *each and every* teacher must be very good. They realize that it is the combination of teachers that makes the difference, learning on top of learning, and that policies must get the whole combination right—initially by establishing high standards, selection procedures that include high academic quality and suitability to teach, job-embedded preparation, and good salaries in line with other graduate professions. Although it will take a while to have the complete effect of changing the profession, early results within a couple of years will provide the necessary confidence and momentum to keep going.

If you look at seven key factors posed by McKinsey & Co. (see Barber & Mourshed, 2007) with respect to their core finding of "developing effective instructors," you will see that they can only occur through collective cultures and processes:

1. What is the total amount of coaching new teachers receive in schools?

2. What preparation of each teacher's time is spent on professional development?

3. Does each teacher have an exact knowledge of specific weaknesses in their practice?

4. Can teachers observe and understand better teaching practice in a school setting?

5. Do teachers reflect on and discuss practice?

6. What role do school leaders play in developing effective instructors?

7. How much focused, systematic research is conducted into effective instruction and then fed back into policy and classroom practice? (Barber & Mourshed, 2007, p. 41)

Barber and his group did not explicitly emphasize that these goals require *collective capacity.* This critical observation was missed or was not appreciated perhaps because it was too implicit. Compound policies apparently require in-your-face clarity because they are more complex than individualistically based policies. A little more complex, but oh so powerful in the consequences.

Once policymakers come to the realization that individual and collective capacity must join in order to get whole-system reform, they immediately know that performance-based merit pay is a non-starter and that charter schools are not the solution but at best a small step along the way—the best charter schools give mainstream schools a wake-up call by furnishing good examples of collective capacity including networking with other schools. Charter schools are only the answer hypothetically if eventually every school becomes a charter school nested in a total system of collaborative competition—something that will never happen through the charter school strategy. We are not going to arrive at the bigger solution by attempting to leverage charter schools (many of which are not particularly good either). The truth is that we must work on the whole system, charter and noncharter alike, immediately to create the capacities that I have been discussing in this book.

This is the same conclusion arrived at by Grubb (2009):

Many of the most effective resources are not improvements of what individuals can make working alone but rather are *collective* resources that can be improved by teachers and leaders working collectively . . . This eliminates [or places serious limitations on] many proposals for improvements in schools that focus only on individuals. (p. 208, emphasis in original)

There is more pressure and support built into transparent, engaged collective cultures than in any hierarchical system I know. There is a way in which collectivities committed to quality are less tolerant of persistently ineffective members, as Bryk and Schneider (2002) and others have found. Indeed, I would say that there are more mechanisms and opportunities for dismissal in the transparent, feedback-laced, results-oriented collective system that I am advocating in this book.

Let's be clear. The strategies I am advocating are designed to improve teacher quality. I am saying that focusing on collective capacity is *essential* if we want to improve the entire profession, which is, after all, the point. (See also Darling-Hammond, 2009, 2010.)

This is a big undertaking for policymakers and the profession. I said that it would take the United States as long as 20 years (although some gains would be noticeable within 2 or 3 years). Finland did it in 30 years; South Korea about the same. I don't know whether it is harder psychologically to be number one, to lose it so definitively, and then to try to reclaim it (the U.S.), or to go from a little to a lot (Finland and Korea). Certainly, the dynamics would be different.

The core agenda is clear—moral purpose and the critical pathways to enact it. One dynamic in our favor, that I have tried to capture in this book, is that we know a great deal more about the small number of compound factors that it will take to make all systems go. We are in a position to generate powerful momentum and gains by focusing on a few good interrelated policies and strategies. Now, if we can only get those damn politicians and unions to cooperate!

PART III
A New Era

CHAPTER SIX

Politicians and Professionals Unite

I won't even attempt the moral-purpose argument. When it comes to democracies, everybody is on the high ground. There is no more room for superiority. Politicians want to get reelected and do good—in that order. Union leaders want to look after their members and do good—again, in that order. But if we can find a way whereby self-interest is met, people will rise to the bigger purpose. In fact, they will embrace the wider goal because to do something good for others is an intrinsically self-satisfying goal for most of us. After basic needs are met, altruism becomes a personal and collective goal that humans find deeply meaningful.

To paraphrase the poet Seamus Heaney, there comes a time in history when moral purpose and self-interest meet. Politicians will have to make the first move, as the people have put them in charge. Recall Premier Dalton McGuinty's (2009) Lesson Three from Chapter 4:

> It doesn't matter how much money you invest; you won't get results *unless teachers are onside* (p. 5, emphasis added).

Teacher unions have a right to be suspicious about government (for example in the U.S. or in Ontario, pre-2003) after years, and in some cases decades, of failed reform where teachers received more blame than the "system" did for failing schools. Now, government has to go out of its way to rebuild relationships with the teaching force. It will take years of persistence, patience, and perspective. It will be frustrating, sometimes desperately slow, but simply put, there is no way to make whole-system reform work without the entire teaching profession and its leaders.

Incidentally, in this book I have not tackled the difficult problem of the role of local school boards. Certainly, many remain dysfunctional, and any change in governance and the role of the state will need to address this perplexing problem (see Maxwell, 2009). The principle of developing collective capacity as it links to raising the bar and closing the gap of student achievement within and across schools must be the driving force in any reconsideration of the role of local school boards.

It is no accident that the 30-year decline in the public school system in the United States coincides exactly with less-than-healthy relationships between unions, governments, and local school boards, although cause and effect is clearly intertwined. Who is going to break the negative cycle? Politicians must initially try to break the deadlock. Those who will be successful will be driven by the vision of creating more equal, prosperous societies. They will also have know-how—strategies with the potential of actually getting there (such as those in this book). Because the goal is so critical and because there is a practical promise of success, strong leaders never, ever give up hope even though the frustrations of getting somewhere, especially at the beginning, can be enormously disheartening. This is one case truly where if there is a will, there is a way.

The will must be founded on the conceptions of reform and how to get there that I have outlined in this book. With respect to governments and professionals, the English in their policy document, Excellence and Fairness: Achieving World Class Public Services (Cabinet Office, England, 2008) call this component of the conception the "new professionalism."

I have made the case, as the Cabinet Office document does, that professionals have to "get the basics right" (p. 28), such as getting the right people into the profession and establishing the conditions for continuous development. The United States especially is not there now. There is important foundation work to be done, and this will require consistency in getting the basics, such as all teachers teaching literacy and numeracy well. It will be an uncomfortable period, as many teachers will have to get basically better.

But, if we know anything from highly successful individuals and organizations it is that relentless consistency in relation to quality goes hand in hand with creativity and innovation. Recall, today's relentless consistency is tomorrow's innovation, and tomorrow's innovation is the next day's relentless consistency. If we get this started right,

> The next stage of public service reform will involve unlocking the creativity and ambition of public sector works and establishing new relationships between the Government and professions. (Cabinet Office, England, 2008, p. 25)

What a compelling, essential prize. Not only do we need teachers onside, we need them being relentlessly competent and innovative. This combination, of course, is exactly required for thriving in our complex, interdependent world—and this is no slogan. To be this good means new relationships between government and professionals. It also means new relationships with parents and the public. The qualified innovative professional knows that parents and the community must be part of the solution, not part of the problem.

If you want to change any relationship, you have to *behave* your way into it. Trust comes after good experiences; first and foremost, politicians are going to have to show the way even if they are not rewarded for it at the start. What would push politicians to take the risks to revamp relationships with unions? Moral purpose is a start. But, so is pressure from the public and education leaders who want a better system. Public confidence, if awakened, generates political willingness to go even further.

The psychology of change at this level is intriguing. Politicians can't get too far ahead (or behind) the public (I thank Ben Levin, 2008, for several of the points here). You have to take people with you, and this means understanding what they think and believe even if you don't agree with it. You have to be prepared to "get down" and talk with people in a respectful way even if they seem uninformed—that's politics. You have to be a learner yourself—humbly confident that you and others can figure it out. You have to respect collective agreements as a starting point. You need clear goals, a storyline, and a keep-on-message approach to keep people onside—25 words or less (Ontario's core goals can be expressed in fewer than 10 words). There is also the need for evidence of results—hence, one important use of test results (provided that they are not excessively narrowly measured). Educators may find the use of test results simplistic, but they work for the public.

If there is any new light coming from the political direction along the lines just described, union leaders are going to have to take some risks. The Albert Shanker of the 21st century is going to be a hero when he or she runs on a platform that says something like,

> We the teachers are in favor of deprivatizing teaching [open the classroom door]; we are in favor of teachers collaborating and learning from each other within and across schools; we support transparency of results and the involvement of citizens; we are deeply committed to all teachers being of high measurable quality, including helping those who are less effective become more effective and counseling out those not suited for the profession; and above all, we the union are deeply committed to working conjointly with the government and the community in order to achieve the moral purpose of raising the bar and closing the gap for each and every child in our society.

After I wrote this statement, there was ever so slightly a glimmer of hope coming from the National Education Association (the largest teacher union in the United States, with 3.2 million members) in a publication with the Center for Teacher Quality with the title, *Children of Poverty Deserve Great Teachers: One Union's Commitment to Change the Status Quo* (Berry, 2009). In that report, NEA commits to four goals: (1) recruit and prepare teachers for high-needs schools, (2) take a comprehensive approach to teacher incentives, (3) improve the right working conditions for teachers, and (4) define *teacher effectiveness* broadly in terms of student learning. But unlike previous reports, this one strays into a new arena with some action steps. The new arena is one where teachers recognize that good school principals are essential; that learning from a critical mass of highly skilled teachers will be required; that a commitment to creative teaching and inquiry learning is basic; and that teachers must *share* a deep commitment to every students' success. And the action steps, albeit baby steps, are to survey the needs of 1,000 high-needs schools and to allocate one million dollars a year for six years to the overall effort. Admittedly, a pittance for a group with 3 million members, but the more important foot in the door is the legitimacy that this report gives to the all-system-go ideas in this book.

But with bad prehistory and urgent moral purpose, things can easily go wrong. Already with the stimulus windfall (one which I said earlier is highly overrated as a solution), there are squabbles that lessen rather than build on the right agenda, such as the recent article in *Education Week,* "NEA at Odds With Obama Team Over 'Race to the Top' Criteria" (Sawchuk, 2009). My point: The "race to the top" money is turning out to be a distractor to the more fundamental goals of transforming the culture of the entire teaching profession. It doesn't matter who is right. You can't make the system go if the teachers as a whole are not onside!

As I said, union leaders need to take some risks, and they should follow the same advice I outlined above: Get the goals right, keep the storyline brief, stay on message, get simple evidence of results, and persist even (especially) if the other side seems obtuse. From a purely self-interest point of view, the windfall for the union and its members would be enormous. You finally become a profession—just like in Finland—right up there with and surpassing doctors, lawyers, and engineers with all the respect and intrinsic and extrinsic rewards that come from it (not that the other professions are always great, but you get the point).

I can't think of a more obvious win-win scenario for both governments and professionals. You both win in just about every measure that counts. Everybody wins, society included. Who is the enemy here? Well, there isn't one except for the inertia of allowing a bad relationship to persist to the detriment of all.

I haven't talked about the "nonschool" factors in this book that will be required to change to truly make *all* systems go. And I will only barely mention them at this point. This is a book about making education systems go. Without getting statistically fancy, I am going to say that if the education sector can get its act together along the lines that I have described, it will solve at least half the problem of equality and prosperity. In statistical language, a quality public education system can reduce the variance in outcomes by half and probably more. Any teacher who has been part of turning around a child, a school, or a district knows that one's address is not one's destiny.

Furthermore, in the chicken-and-egg sense, altering one variable—education—can improve another variable—a better life. But, we still need to explicitly work on key nonschool factors. One powerful set that we are about to tackle, and one that straddles school and nonschool factors, is early care and learning

(Ontario Government, 2009). In this Pascal report (named after the advisor who was commissioned to produce it), the government has first committed to all-day integrated care and learning for all four- and five-year-olds based in the school setting. It will be phased in starting in 2010, but when fully implemented, parents who want all day, 7:30 AM to 6 PM, care and best start for learning will be able to get it. This will lead to best start family centers in which nutritional, health, emotional, and cognitive development needs of all children ages 4 through 12 will be addressed. Beyond that, extended parent leave (for mothers and fathers) will be established in the future. At the same time, services are needed for the prenatal to age-3 children.

This, in turn, leads to parenting skills, the question of early vocabulary growth—in which children with parents more highly educated get exposed to triple the number of words than working class or parents on social assistance—and so on.

Similarly, Grubb (2009, pp. 284–285) has listed nine domains of action relative to nonschool strategies and progress, including early childhood practices, income support, full range of health services, family support, and others.

Another great source is Susan Neuman's (2009) analysis of the essential principles of high-quality progress that "change the odds for children at risk." Her book goes into the most detail on the range of early care, after-hours and community-based programs that are already working, albeit in pockets, around the United States. Neuman ends her book on the same tone as this chapter—"accept no excuses," she says (p. 187).

But this book is about making the education system go. We know what it looks like and how to do it. It does take will and a no-excuses perseverance along with know-how—resolute leadership at all levels. I have said that the role of governments is to set the direction, even in an assertive way, and then—crucially—to engage in the two-way partnerships necessary to resolve problems and to develop individual and collective capacity as linked to measurable results on a small number of key priorities. Other levels of the sector, districts and schools, must become more proactive with respect to the new agenda, engaging vertically and horizontally in purposeful networks. Put differently, local levels need to "exploit" (in the most positive sense of this word) policies for the betterment of their students. The new policies I am recommending will direct and shape the next phase, but they need not be experienced as restrictive. There is plenty of room for active claiming of the agenda.

This agenda, as I have argued, must go beyond standards, assessment, and accountability. The missing component is the focus on *instruction* and building the associated individual and collective capacity to improve all classrooms, schools, and school systems. This has been the United States' very weakest suit in the 45 years since 1965 when the country first got into the business of deliberate improvement through federal and state policy (Cohen and Moffitt, 2009).

The evidence is overwhelming that we need a social or collective solution. If the reader needs any more convincing, consider Tony Bryk and colleagues' (2010) careful, detailed longitudinal study of school improvement in Chicago schools since 1989. In comparing over 100 schools that had improved over the years (in reading, mathematics, and other measures) with over 100 schools that had stagnated or declined, Bryk et al. found five key factors that accounted for the differences: (1) school leadership (the principal) as driver who works with teachers, students, parents, and the community to build, in turn, four other interrelated focuses and supports—(2) parent and community ties, (3) professional capacity of staff (including focused work orientation), (4) a student-centered learning climate, and (5) instructional focus and guidance (p. 82)—all terms we are familiar with in *All Systems Go* from previous chapters.

Schools that had these capacities were 10 times more likely to be successful in improving student engagement and learning. Put another way, no schools that were weak on these factors improved (Bryk et al., 2010, p. 117)—not one school! I said in the preface that the single most important thing to remember in *All Systems Go* is that the solution unequivocally consists of increasing *collective capacity*. Bryk et al. underscored this crucial finding: "the results presented here document one important fact: curriculum alignment is a *social* activity as well as a technical act. Its development entails sustained work among teachers within and across grades" (p. 117, emphasis added).

Bryk et al. (2010) did not find "systemic success" in Chicago. Over 100 schools is a lot but it is less than 20% of the schools in the district. Still the point remains, you can't get anywhere without developing collective capacity focused on a small core of key interrelated factors. In a phrase, you cannot make the system go unless you make collective engagement *the* priority. The evidence for this conclusion is overwhelming. It is not easy, but it is doable. Every successful school and system in the world proves the point that only collective engagement will get us the results we are seeking.

As we examine how education systems in the world become highly successful, I am confident that the analysis and recommendations in this book will be validated. The new McKinsey and Co. report (as yet untitled) that identifies the characteristics of the 20 or so countries that have promising or sustainable results should add to our store of convincing policies and strategies that work. These reports will always show that the agendas of the government and the teaching profession must converge—for the good of society and for their own good.

Thus, the missing link is the powerhouse force of collective capacity building and efficacy. There is no force so durable and potent as a social force. It has it all. Competencies and skills increase, quality and innovation occur hand in hand, and gale-force commitment occurs because peers commit to peers and hierarchies become flatlined in their interactions.

This is a time in history when one's self-interest and the collective good overlap substantially. If we expect people to send us their children and give us billions of dollars, we must get our act together and deliver value. But it is more than that. There is no greater secular calling than having the opportunity to improve one's self and others—with, as we have seen, countless benefits for individuals and society. The all-systems-go agenda is worth uniting on because it simultaneously transcends and gives meaning to life—a union on earth.

References

Alliance for Excellent Education. (2008). *Dropouts, diplomas, and dollars.* Washington, DC: Author.

Austin, J., Grossman, A., Schwartz, R., & Suesse, J. (2004). *Long Beach Unified School District: Change that leads to improvement (1992–2002).* Cambridge, MA: Public Education Leadership Project at Harvard University.

Austin, J., Grossman, A., Schwartz, R., & Suesse, J. (2006). *Managing at scale in the Long Beach Unified District.* Cambridge, MA: Public Education Leadership Project at Harvard University.

Barber, M. (2008). *Instruction to deliver.* London: Methuen.

Barber, M., & Mourshed, M. (2007). *How the world's best-performing school systems come out on top.* London: McKinsey & Co.

Berry, B. (2009). *Children of poverty deserve great teachers: One union's commitment to change the status quo.* Hillsborough, NC: Center for Teacher Quality and Washington, DC: National Education Association.

Boyle, A. (2009). *Tower Hamlets case story.* Unpublished paper, Beyond Expectations Project, Boston College.

Bryk, A., Bender-Sebring, P., Allensworth, E., Luppescu, S., & Easton, J. (2010). *Organizing schools for improvement: Lessons from Chicago.* Chicago: University of Chicago Press.

Bryk, A., & Schneider, B. (2002). *Trust in schools.* New York: Russell Sage.

Cabinet Office, England. (2008). *Excellence and fairness: Achieving world class public services.* London: Author.

Campbell, D. (1979). Assessing the impact of planned social change. *Education and Program Planning, 2,* 67–90.

Center on Education Policy (2009). *An early look at the economic stimulus package and the public schools: Perspectives from state leaders.* Washington, DC: Author.

Childress, S. (2009). Moving beyond the conventional wisdom of whole-district reform. *Education Week, 29*(4), 30–31.

Cisco, Intel, & Microsoft. (2009). Transforming education: Assessing and teaching 21st century skills. Melbourne, Australia: Author.

Cohen, D., & Moffitt, S. (2009). *The ordeal of equality: Did federal regulation fix the school?* Cambridge, MA: Harvard University Press.

Corcoran, S., Schwartz, A., & Weinstein, M. (2009). *The New York City aspiring principals' program.* New York: Institute for Education and Social Policy, New York University.

Crawford, M. (2009). *Shop class as soulcraft.* New York: Penguin Press.

Darling-Hammond, L. (2009). Teaching and change wars: The professional hypothesis. In A. Hargreaves & M. Fullan (Eds.), *Change wars* (pp. 45–70). Bloomington, IN: Solution Tree.

Darling-Hammond, L. (2010). *The flat world and education: How America's commitment to equity will determine our future.* New York: Teachers College Press.

Darling-Hammond, L., Meyerson, D., LaPointe, M., & Orr, M. (2010). *Preparing school leaders for a changing world.* San Francisco: Jossey-Bass.

Dufour, R., Dufour, R., Eaker, R., & Karhanek, G. (2010). *Raising the bar, closing the gap: Whatever it takes.* Bloomington, ID: Solution Tree.

Duncan, A. (2009, June 14). *States will lead the way toward reform.* Speech to National Governors Association, Washington, DC.

Education Quality and Accountability Office. (2009). *Primary division, junior division and grade 9 results.* Toronto, Ontario: Author.

Education Week. (2009). *The Obama education plan.* San Francisco: Jossey-Bass.

Elmore, R. (2004). *School reform from the inside out.* Cambridge, MA: Harvard University Press.

Elmore, R., & Burney, D. (1999). Investing in teacher learning. In L. Darling-Hammond & G. Sykes (Eds.), *Teaching as a learning profession* (pp. 236–291). San Francisco: Jossey-Bass.

Fullan, M. (2007). *The new meaning of educational change.* New York: Teachers College Press.

Fullan, M. (2008). *The six secrets of change.* San Francisco: Jossey-Bass.

Fullan, M. (2009). Leadership development: The larger context. *Education Leadership (67)*2, 45–49.

Fullan, M. (2010). *Motion leadership: The skinny on becoming change savvy.* Thousand Oaks, CA: Corwin.

Fullan, M. (forthcoming). *Motion leadership: The movie* [Motion picture]. Salt Lake City, UT: School Improvement Network, and Thousand Oaks, CA: Corwin.

Grubb, W. N. (2009). *The money myth.* New York: Russell Sage Foundation.

Hansen, M. (2009). *Collaboration: How leaders avoid the traps, create unity, and reap big results.* Boston: Harvard Business Press.

Hanushek, E., & Lindseth, A. (2009). *Schoolhouses, courthouses and statehouses.* Princeton, NJ: Princeton University Press.

Hargreaves, A., & Shirley, D. (2009). *The fourth way.* Thousand Oaks, CA: Corwin.

Hattie, J. (2009). *Visible learning.* London: Routledge.

Homer-Dixon, T. (2009, August 8). Environmental sustainability. *Toronto Globe & Mail*, p. A15.

Hopper, K., & Hopper, W. (2009). *The puritan gift*. London: I. B. Tauris.

Johnson, S. M. (2004). *Finders and keepers: Helping new teachers thrive and survive in our schools*. San Francisco: Jossey-Bass.

Johnson, S. M., & Papay, J. (2009). *Redesigning teacher pay*. Washington, DC: Economic Policy Institute.

Leithwood, K. (2007). *Teacher working conditions that matter: A synthesis of evidence*. Toronto: Elementary Teacher Federation of Ontario.

Leithwood, K., Harris, A., & Strauss, T. (2010). *Leadership for turning schools around*. San Francisco: Jossey-Bass.

Leithwood, K., & Jantzi, D. (2008). *Evaluation of the project: Leading student achievement: Our principal purpose*. Toronto: Ontario Institute for Studies in Education.

Levin, B. (2008). *How to change 5,000 schools*. Cambridge, MA: Harvard Education Press.

Louis, K., Leithwood, K., Wahlstrom, K., Anderson, S., Michlin, M., Mascall, B., et al. (2009). *Learning from districts' efforts to improve student achievement*. New York: Wallace Foundation.

Martins, P. (2009). *Individual teacher incentives, student achievement and grade inflation*. Bonn, Germany: Institute for the Study of Labor.

Maxwell, L. (2009). An overlooked institution struggles to remain relevant. *Education Week, (29)*7, 3–5.

McGuinty, D. (2009, June 30). *Remarks on lessons learned*. Keynote address presented at the Global Education Competitiveness Summit, Washington, DC.

McKinsey & Co. (2009). *The economic impact of the achievement gap in America's schools*. Washington, DC: Author.

McNeil, M. (2009). Hurdles ahead in 'race to the top.' *Education Week, (29)*1, p. 1–22.

Mintzberg, H. (2004). *Managers not MBAs*. San Francisco: Berrett-Koehler.

National Commission on Excellence in Education. (1983). *A nation at risk*. Washington, DC: U.S. Government Printing Office.

Neuman, S. (2009). *Changing the odds for children at risk*. Westport, CT: Praeger.

Ontario Government. (2009). *With our best future in mind: Implementing early learning in Ontario*. Toronto, Ontario: Report to the Premier by the Special Advisor on Early Learning, Charles Pascal.

Ottawa Catholic School Board. (2009). *Senior kindergarten tutoring program: Program evaluation report*. Ottawa, Canada: Author.

Pfeffer, J., & Sutton, R. (2006). *Hard facts, dangerous half-truths and total nonsense*. Boston: Harvard Business School Press.

Reeves, D. (2010). *Finding your leadership focus*. New York: Teachers College Press.

Rothstein, R., Jacobsen, R., & Wilder, T. (2008). *Grading education: Getting accountability right*. Washington, DC: Economic Policy Institute and New York: Teachers College Press.

Sawchuk, S. (2009). NEA at odds with Obama team over 'race to the top' criteria. *Education Week, (29)*2, p. 6.

Schleicher, A. (2009a, June 22). *Assessing educational performance internationally*. Presentation given to the Commission on State School Officers, San Francisco.

Schleicher, A. (2009b). *Lessons from the world on effective teaching and learning environments*. Paris: OECD, unpublished paper.

Sharratt, L., & Fullan, M. (2009). *Realization: The change imperative for deepening district-wide reform*. Thousand Oaks, CA: Corwin.

Springer, M. (2009). *Performance incentives*. Washington, DC: Brookings Institution Press.

Trilling, B., & Fadel, C. (2009). *21st century skills: Learning for life in our times*. San Francisco: Jossey-Bass.

U.S. Department of Education. (2009). *Race to the top program: Executive summary*. Washington, DC: Author.

Vallas, P., & Jacobs, L. (2009). 'Race to the top' lessons from New Orleans. *Education Week, (29)*2, 26–27.

Viadero, D. (2009). Teacher compensation ripe for change, authors say. *Education Week, (29)*7, 10.

Whelan, F. (2009). *Lessons learned: How good policies produce better schools*. London: Fenton Whelan.

Wilkinson, R., & Pickett, R. (2009). *The spirit level: Why more equal societies almost always do better*. London: Allen P-Lane.

Yarrow, A. (2009). State of mind: America's teaching corps. *Education Week, (29)*8, 21–23.

Index

Academic achievement:
  collective capacity building, 74–75
  district-level reform, 37, 48, 53
  four-level implementation audit
    scale, 55
  intelligent accountability, 68–70
  international research, 15–18
  literacy proficiency, 7–8, 13–14,
    37, 45, 46–47, 48, 53
  mathematics, 14, 45, 47, 53, 74–75
  numeracy proficiency, 13–14,
    45, 46–47
  reading, 14, 20, 45, 47, 53, 74–75
  school-level reform, 7–8, 45, 46–47
  social impact, 15–18
  state-level reform, 14, 74–75
  writing, 14, 45, 47, 53, 74–75
Academic achievement gap:
  international research, 16–17
  racial disparities, 16
Academic assessment:
  international, 15, 19–20, 57, 80
  literacy, 8, 11, 15–16
  mathematics, 15–16
  science, 15–16
  value-added assessments, 27
Adlai Stevenson High School,
  Illinois, 54, 55
African Americans, 16
Allegiance, district-level
  reform, 37, 38
All-systems-go strategy:
  collective capacity building,
    61 (exhibit), 71–77
  component overview, 61 (exhibit)

district-level reform, 12
federal-level reform, 78–80
intelligent accountability,
  61 (exhibit), 66–70
moral purpose, 61 (exhibit),
  62–63, 76–77
resolute leadership, 61 (exhibit),
  64–66
school-level reform, 6
state-level reform, 13, 62–78
whole-system reform, 3–5
Alvarado, Tony, 42
American Reinvestment and
  Recovery Act (ARRA), 29, 30–31
Armadale Public School, Toronto,
  Ontario, Canada, 45–47
"Assessing and Teaching 21st
  Century Skills" (CISCO,
  Intel, & Microsoft), 20
Assessment. *See* Academic
  assessment
Australia, 15, 16, 80

Bangladeshi immigrants, 37, 39–40
Bersin, Alan, 42
Beyond Expectations (Hargreaves &
  Harris), 37
Boones Elementary, Virginia, 54
Buddy-day strategy, 7, 51
Bush, George H. W., 22
Bush, George W., 22

California, 32, 40–43, 54, 56
Canada. *See* Ontario, Canada;
  specific district/school

Catholic districts. *See* Ottawa Catholic District School Board, Ontario, Canada
Center for Education Policy, 30–31
Center for Teacher Quality, 98
Charter schools, 91
Cinco Ranch High School, Texas, 54
CISCO, 20
City Academy, 40
Class size reduction, 20–21, 42
Cohn, Carl, 40–42
Collaborative competition:
    district-level reform, 12, 38, 41
    state-level reform, 15
    whole-system reform, 5
Collective capacity building:
    academic achievement, 74–75
    district-level reform, 12, 43–45
    individual capacity building, 61 (exhibit), 77–78, 87–89, 91–92
    intelligent accountability, 68–70
    resources, 71–72
    school-level reform, 6–7, 11, 12, 45–47
    social glue, 47, 50–51
    state-level reform, 13–15, 61 (exhibit), 71–77
    whole-system reform, 4–5
Collective efficacy, district-level reform, 44–45
Collins, Kevan, 39
Complex resources, 20–21, 25, 71
Compound resources, 20, 25, 71–72
Core priorities, 4
Crawford, M., 10
Creativity, 10, 20
Credit-recovery program, 9
Credit-rescue program, 9
Critical learning pathways model, 14
Critical thinking skills, 4, 19–20
Crosby Heights, Toronto, Ontario, Canada, 45
Curriculum Services Canada, 74

Data walls, 7
Decentralized management, 31–32
Disciplined collaboration, 5

District-level reform:
    allegiance, 37, 38
    all-systems-go strategy, 12
    challenges to, 56–59
    collaborative competition, 12, 38, 41
    collective capacity building, 12, 43–45
    collective efficacy, 44–45
    effective characteristics, 36 (exhibit)
    individual capacity building, 12
    instructional feedback, 41
    intelligent accountability, 43–44, 48–49
    job-embedded professional learning, 46
    lateral capacity building, 12–13
    leadership, 12
    literacy proficiency, 37, 48, 53
    Long Beach Unified School District (LBUSD), California, 40–43
    moral purpose, 12, 38, 43, 54
    Ottawa Catholic District School Board, Ontario, Canada, 49–55
    personnel policies, 12, 49, 52–53
    precision strategies, 46, 51–52
    professional power, 37, 39
    resolute leadership, 37–38
    specificity, 46
    sustainability, 37, 39–40, 43, 48–49
    sustainable realization, 43, 48–49
    Tower Hamlets, London, England, 37–40
    transparency, 12
    York Region District School Board (YRDSB), Toronto, Ontario, Canada, 43–49
Domain knowledge, 73
Duncan, Arne, 28–30, 32, 78–79
Dynamic inequality, 57–58

Early-learning initiative, 8
Education Quality and Accountability Office (EQAO) (Canada), 45, 68, 74–75

Engagement coach, 52
England, 17, 37–40, 66

Federal-level reform:
    frame-and-deliver strategy, 78–80
    legislation, 4, 21–26, 29,
        30–31, 70, 80
    new professionalism, 96
    nonschool factors, 99–100
    professional partnership, 95–101
    state partnership, 78–80
    teacher unions, 95–99
Feedback:
    district-level reform, 41
    school-level reform, 7
Finland, 16
Four-pillar plan, 28–30
    international benchmarked
        standards, 29, 62
    robust data system, 28, 29
    state reform agenda, 30–31
    teacher quality, 28, 30
    turnaround-schools strategy,
        29, 30
French-language Education
    Policy and Programs Branch
    (FLEPPB), 76
Friedman, Ryan, 45

Gersten, Lewis, 82
Gilbert, Christine, 38, 39
Global Education Competitiveness
    Summit, Washington, D.C.,
    2009, 64
Grier, Terry, 42–43
Gross domestic product (GDP), 16

*Hard Facts, Dangerous Half-Truths
    and Total Nonsense* (Pfeffer
    and Sutton), 83
Hargreaves, A., 37
Harris, A., 37
Highland Elementary School,
    Maryland, 54
High school dropout rate, 16
High school graduation rate:
    school-level reform, 11
    state-level reform, 13–14

High skills major (HSM), 9–11
Hogarth, Bill, 43, 48

IBM, 82
Illinois, 54, 55
Inclusionary programs, 4
Income inequality, 16–18
Individual capacity building:
    collective capacity building, 61
        (exhibit), 77–78, 87–89, 91–92
    critique of, 82–86
    district-level reform, 12
    job-embedded professional
        learning, 85–86
    moral purpose, 90–92
    performance pay, 82–85, 86–89, 91
    policy strategies, 89–92
    positive perspective of, 86–89
    state-level reform, 14–15,
        61 (exhibit), 77–78, 89–92
    teacher quality, 86–89
Intel Corporation, 20
Intellectual engagement, 10
Intelligent accountability:
    academic achievement, 68–70
    collective capacity building, 68–70
    district-level reform, 43–44, 48–49
    internal accountability, 57,
        66 (exhibit), 67–70
    performance-based funding
        system, 26–27
    principles of, 66 (exhibit)
    state-level reform, 61 (exhibit), 66–70
    whole-system reform, 4 (exhibit), 5
Internal accountability, 57,
    66 (exhibit), 67–70
International assessments,
    15, 19–20, 57, 80
International benchmarked
    standards, 29, 62
International research:
    academic achievement, 15–18
    academic achievement gap, 16–17
    income inequality, 16–18

Job-embedded professional learning:
    district-level reform, 46
    individual capacity building, 85–86

Kansas, 54
Kansas City, Missouri,
     School District (KCMSD), 25
Kildeer Elementary School
     District 96, Illinois, 54, 55
Korea, 16

Lakeridge Junior High School,
     Utah, 54
Lateral capacity building, 12–13
Latinos, 16
Leading school achievement (LSA)
     project, 74
Learning network (LN), 47–48,
     52, 72–74
Legislative reform, 4, 21–26, 29,
     30–31, 70, 80
Literacy assessment:
   school-level reform, 8, 11
   social impact, 15–16
Literacy coach, 7
Literacy proficiency:
   district-level reform, 37, 48, 53
   school-level reform, 7–8, 45, 46–47
   state-level reform, 13–14
Litigation, 25
Long Beach Unified School District
     (LBUSD), California, 40–43
   collaborative competition, 41
   district structure, 40
   state-level reform, 42
   student demographics, 40

Management, 31–32
Many, Tom, 55
Marr, Jill, 45–46
Maryland, 54, 56
Mathematics:
   academic achievement,
      14, 45, 47, 53, 74–75
   assessment of, 15–16
   state-level reform, 14, 74–75
McCracken, Jamie, 49–53
McGuinty, Dalton, 64, 95
Merit pay. See Performance pay
Microsoft, 20
Miliband, David, 66
Missouri, 25

Money-plus resources, 20
Moral purpose/high expectations:
   district-level reform, 12, 38, 43, 54
   individual capacity building, 90–92
   state-level reform, 61 (exhibit),
      62–63, 76–77

National Board for Professional
     Teaching, 87
National Education Association, 98
New Orleans, 31–32
New professionalism, 96
New York City, District 2, 31–32,
     35, 42
No Child Left Behind (NCLB)
     Act (2002), 4, 21–26, 80
Numeracy proficiency:
   school-level reform, 45, 46–47
   state-level reform, 13–14

Obama, Barack, 28, 32
Ontario, Canada:
   district-level reform, 43–55
   school district demographics, 13
Ontario Focused Intervention
     Partnership (OFIP), 14, 68–70
Ontario Literacy and Numeracy
     Secretariat, 13, 14, 69, 73–74
Ontario Ministry of Education, 13, 73
Ontario Secondary School Literacy
     Test (OSSLT), 8, 11
Organization for Economic
     Cooperation and Development
     (OECD), 15, 19–20, 57, 80
Ottawa Catholic District School
     Board, Ontario, Canada, 49–55
   buddy-day strategy, 51
   district structure, 50
   learning network (LN), 52, 72
   moral purpose, 54
   personnel policies, 52–53
   precision strategies, 51–52
   reimagining days, 50
   school engagement project, 51–52
   Senior Kindergarten Tutoring
      Program, 52
   skinny rules, 50–51
   social justice fund, 53

Peer Literacy and Numeracy
    Tutoring (PLANT), 8
Performance-based funding
    system, 26–28
    accountability, 26–27
    assessment, 26
    continuous improvement, 26, 28
    evaluation, 26, 28
    information, 26, 28
    local decision-making, 26, 2727
    rational/equitable funding, 26, 28
    rewards-incentives, 26, 27
    standards, 26
Performance pay, 27, 82–85,
    86–89, 91
Personnel policies, district-level
    reform, 12, 49, 52–53
Pfeffer, J., 83
Portugal, 84
Prairie Star Middle School,
    Kansas, 54
Precision strategies:
    district-level reform, 46, 51–52
    whole-system reform, 4 (exhibit), 5
Problem-solving skills, 4, 19–20
Professional development. *See*
    Teacher quality
Professional power, district-level
    reform, 37, 39
Programme for International Student
    Assessment (PISA),
    15, 19–20, 57, 80
Provincial Interest Regulation
    (Ontario, Canada), 70

Quality teachers. *See* Teacher quality

Race to the Top (R2T), 29, 30,
    32, 79, 99
Racial differences, 16
Reading:
    academic achievement, 14, 20,
        45, 47, 53, 74–75
    state-level reform, 14, 74–75
Rescue-and-recovery courses, 8–9
Resolute leadership:
    district-level reform, 37–38
    message sustainability, 4

state-level reform,
    13, 61 (exhibit), 64–66
    whole-system reform, 4
Resources:
    collective capacity building, 71–72
    complex resources, 20–21, 25, 71
    compound resources, 20, 25,
        71–72
    money-plus, 20
    simple resources, 20, 25–26,
        42, 71

San Diego City School District,
    California, 42–43
Sanger Unified School District,
    California, 54, 55
Schleicher, Andreas, 15, 57
School boards, 96
School-level reform:
    academic achievement, 7–8,
        45, 46–47
    all-systems-go strategy, 6
    buddy-day strategy, 7, 51
    case studies, 5–12
    change agents, 6
    collective capacity building,
        6–7, 11, 12, 45–47
    credit-recovery program, 9
    credit-rescue program, 9
    early-learning initiative, 8
    feedback, 7, 58
    high school graduation rate, 11
    high skills major (HSM), 9–11
    instructional quality, 6–7
    literacy coach, 7
    rescue-and-recovery courses, 8–9
    student success teacher (SST),
        8–9, 11
Schools on the Move, 14
Science assessment, 15–16
Senior Kindergarten Tutoring
    Program, Canada, 52
Sharratt, Lyn, 43
Shop Class as Soul Craft (Crawford), 10
Simple resources, 20, 25–26, 42, 71
Social equity, 16–18
Social impact, 15–18
Social justice fund, 53

Specificity:
  district-level reform, 46
  whole-system reform, 5
State-level reform:
  academic achievement, 14
  all-systems-go strategy, 13, 62–78
  collaborative competition, 15
  collective capacity building,
        13–15, 61 (exhibit), 71–77
  critical learning pathways model, 14
  domain knowledge, 73
  examples of, 14
  federal partnership, 78–80
  four-pillar plan, 30–31
  high school graduation rate, 13–14
  individual capacity building,
        14–15, 61 (exhibit),
        77–78, 89–92
  intelligent accountability,
        61 (exhibit), 66–70
  literacy proficiency, 13–14
  moral purpose, 61 (exhibit),
        62–63, 76–77
  numeracy proficiency, 13–14
  resolute leadership,
        13, 61 (exhibit), 64–66
  Schools on the Move, 14
  student success (SS) group, 13, 73
  transparency, 77, 92
  turnaround-schools strategy,
        14, 68
"State Success Factor" (U.S.
    Department of Education),
    30–31
Student success (SS) group, 13, 73
Student success teacher (SST),
    8–9, 11
Sustainability, district-level reform,
    37, 39–40, 43, 48–49
Sustainable realization, 43, 48–49
Sutton, R., 83
Sweden, 16, 17

Teacher effectiveness, 98
Teacher quality:
  contented teachers, 88
  disheartened teachers, 88
  four-pillar plan, 28, 30
  idealist teachers, 88
  incentives for, 86–89
  individual capacity building, 86–89
  performance pay, 27, 82–85,
        86–89, 91
  school-level reform, 6–7, 58
  seven practicalities, 88
Teacher unions, 95–99
Texas, 32, 54
Tower Hamlets, London,
        England, 37–40
  allegiance, 37, 38
  collaborative competition, 38
  moral purpose, 38
  professional power, 37, 39
  resolute leadership, 37–38
  student demographics, 37
  sustainability, 37, 39–40
Transparency:
  district-level reform, 12
  performance-based funding
        system, 27
  state-level reform, 77, 92
Turnaround-schools strategy:
  four-pillar plan, 29, 30
  state-level reform, 14, 68
Tutoring, 8, 52

Unions, 95–99
Utah, 54

Value-added assessments, 27
Virginia, 54

Wales, 17
Wallace Foundation, 44
Whittier Union High School
        District, California, 54
Whole-system reform:
  all-systems-go strategy, 3–5
  case studies, 5–15
  guiding principles, 3–5
  higher order skills, 19–20
  lessons learned, 64–66
  levels of, 5–15
  overview, 4 (exhibit)
  resources, 19, 20–21
  social impact, 15–18

successful elements of, 21 (exhibit)
See also District-level reform; School-
level reform; State-level reform
Whole-system reform inadequacies,
21–32
decentralized management, 31–32
four-pillar plan, 28–30, 62
funding, 21–22, 23, 26–28
legislative reform, 21–26, 80
litigation, 25
performance-based funding
system, 26–28
wasted resources, 23–26
Writing:
academic achievement, 14, 45, 47,
53, 74–75
state-level reform, 14, 74–75

York Region District School Board
(YRDSB), Toronto, Ontario,
Canada, 43–49
allegiances, 45, 48
collaborative competition, 45, 48
collective capacity building,
43–45
collective efficacy, 44–45
district structure, 43
individual capacity building, 49
intelligent accountability, 43–44,
48–49
job-embedded professional
learning, 46
learning network (LN), 47–48, 52,
72–74
moral purpose, 43
personnel policies, 49
precision strategies, 46
professional learning, 46, 47–48
specificity, 46
sustainability, 48–49
sustainable realization,
43, 48–49

CORWIN
A SAGE Company

The Corwin logo—a raven striding across an open book—represents the union of courage and learning. Corwin is committed to improving education for all learners by publishing books and other professional development resources for those serving the field of PreK–12 education. By providing practical, hands-on materials, Corwin continues to carry out the promise of its motto: **"Helping Educators Do Their Work Better."**

ONTARIO
PRINCIPALS'
COUNCIL

The Ontario Principals' Council (OPC) is a voluntary professional association for principals and vice-principals in Ontario's public school system. We believe that exemplary leadership results in outstanding schools and improved student achievement. To this end, we foster quality leadership through world-class professional services and supports. As an ISO 9001 registered organization, we are committed to our statement that "quality leadership is our principal product."